INFORMED DIVORCE

FACING THE FUTURE WITH A PLAN

JOHN P. CANNON

CANNON & ASSOCIATES

YOUR FIERCE ADVOCATES®

DISCLAIMER

Nothing contained in this book shall be considered rendering legal advice for specific cases or legal issues. Readers are responsible for obtaining legal advice from legal counsel licensed in their own state and experienced in the legal issue the reader is facing. This book and any resources provided are intended for educational and informational purposes only.

The materials contained herein represent the author's opinions and should not be consulted to be the action of either Cannon & Associates or any government official.

CONTENTS

CLIENT TESTIMONIALS

"I cannot say enough about John and his team. They are knowledgeable and thoroughly professional. You definitely want them in your corner if you have been arrested or find yourself heading to family court. Top notch!"

Debra

"Cannon & Associates is the best and took so much stress out of the very difficult situation I was put in. Erick Harris represented me in my divorce and did an amazing job. He made it very easy for me, made sure I was taken care of, and most importantly made sure my children were kept safe. The entire staff is very welcoming and will go above and beyond for everyone."

Jamez

"This attorney has helped me so much and is fighting tooth and nail to help me win custody for my son. I've explained the situation and he has taken this case very professionally. I wouldn't hire any other lawyer as Mr. Cannon has keyed my case to perfection and has given me the best options of opportunity with my son in this case from the beginning. I would honestly give him a 10★ Rating if Google would allow me. Hands down I would recommend Mr. Cannon in any court situation for any case you may be struggling with. This is by far the best attorney and gives satisfaction and every option available during court. I admire what he has done for me and my family."

Steve

"I highly recommend Cannon & Associates to anyone in need of an attorney for any reason. If they are unable to take your case, they assist you in finding someone who can. I want to personally thank Kelly for her quick response in helping me and my family get the attorney we needed and the continued contact to make sure we were doing well. That true care for people is hard to find in attorney's and this law firm absolutely cares. THANK YOU SO VERY MUCH!!"

Luann

"Erick Harris and Lisa Smith are a dynamic duo! Erick Harris was an exceptional advocate for me in an extremely sensitive international case, that required them to effectively work with legal counsel outside of the US. They worked with local magistrates to bypass complex international conventions that would normally not only increase the turnaround of my case but also the number of parties involved, the cost, and the complexity. Their work was very honest and transparent and professional, even at times when I was not an easy client to manage. Prior to Erick and Lisa, I had retained counsel from another law firm, spoken with numerous others, and finally spoke with Lisa Smith who immediately understood my situation and intentions so well that she could complete the sentence that I was saying to her, other legal advisors were pondering whether or not my intentions were even possible. I highly recommend Erick and Lisa!"

Ronald

Tom Stone and the team at Cannon & Associates are a solid group for family law matters. Cool headed representation prevails as emotions escalate in difficult **divorce** matters.

Robert

John Cannon has helped me through the hardest time in my life. He helped me through my **divorce** and custody case. He truly cares about his clients and it made me so happy he always put my daughter first and wanted what was in her best interest as a child. He is very sharp and resourceful and he has been very attentive and responsive to my needs, John is very polite and professional and he always has a great attitude. John always took the time to go over everything and explain everything in depth. I've enjoyed working with John and his team and would recommend him to other clients.

Lexi

5 out of 5 would recommend John and his team for **divorce**. This group takes care of families and does everything they can to move your case along as smoothly and efficiently as possible.

Hannah

Mr. Cannon was exceedingly professional and friendly. I was most impressed with his timely follow-up and feedback via email and phone. Throughout the **divorce** process, Mr. Cannon helped direct and lead with expert advise and trustworthy management through all legalities.

Mark

EXCELLENT law firm, HIGHLY recommend. You can't beat the expertise of John Cannon! When we called the office for help Shelley, Angelia, and Kelly were very compassionate and professional during the intake process. After obtaining detailed information to identify what our specific legal needs were, we were quoted a price and payment options. It was determined which Attorney would best suit our situation and we were paired up with the Attorney's Paralegal to get things started. Our Paralegal was excellent, kind, communicative and responsive to all of our needs and inquiries. John Cannon was articulate, informative, and handled the case like the amazing PRO that he is! Thank you so much to Mr. Cannon and the entire professional Team that stands behind him.

Kathy

SECTION 1: INTRODUCTION

"Cannon and Associates is an extremely professional and detailed Law firm. In addition, our Attorney and Paralegal was a well-coordinated team embracing us like family with kindness and confidence every step of the way. I could not be happier with our choice as well as the outcomes they provided. They will be our first choice for our legal needs."

Thomas

Confusion, frustration, panic. These feelings are common for anyone facing the end of a marriage. If your divorce is imminent or already underway, you have two choices:

- get swept up in the process and hope for the best, or
- learn about your rights and how to protect them.

If you are ready to learn to be a courageous, assertive actor in shaping **Your Better Future Now**, this book is for you. This book is a guide to those facing the range of issues that arise before and during family law litigation.

This book is not an all-encompassing treatise on all areas of family law, as that would span over a thousand pages. Instead, this guidebook has three main purposes:

1. To educate those facing divorce and child custody matters.

2. To help you evaluate and identify the best family law attorney for you.

3. To comfort you along the road ahead, as "knowledge is power."

Learning the Issues

Divorcing is not always easy. You may already feel overwhelmed by the sheer number of decisions and potential changes divorce will bring about in your life and, if you have any, in your children's lives. The issues involved in family law are some of the most emotionally and mentally taxing that we experience in our lives. It may help to know that you are not the first or only person who has faced divorce. This book is based on working with thousands of clients whom we helped manage their emotional and mental demands to obtain their desired outcomes. Whether it's the first time you're admitting divorce is a possibility or the final stages of entering a divorce settlement, this book can give you clarity.

Obtaining a divorce decree does not always have to be difficult. You may feel bewildered as you try to figure out court papers or online legal codes on your own. Even though every divorce is different, divorce laws and family courts have procedures and rules that allow those involved in divorce insight into possible outcomes. Decisions in family law are based on various factors, some of which may not occur to you until it's too late. This book is based on our decades of experience working in family law and with family courts. Whether your situation seems straightforward or exhaustingly complicated, this book can help you avoid unpleasant surprises.

Choosing Your Attorney

As I explain throughout this book, family law litigation is a fascinating combination of individual psychology, strategic negotiation, accounting, and communication.

Psychology is a second calling for most family lawyers, as family law cases are packed with intense emotions and fears. Experienced family lawyers understand the dynamics in each client's case and the psychological impact of the marriage or relationship ending. Working with clients facing emotional pain and suffering is challenging and requires an attorney who can coach each client through one of the most difficult times in life.

Strategic negotiation is a skill acquired with preparation and practice. Family lawyers must be strategic in their interactions with opposing counsel and the court at every turn. Contested family law cases are more like a chess match than a battle. Therefore, experienced family law attorneys and divorce attorneys study their opponents, the judges, and the law to make the best possible move at each step in your case. Understanding the law and procedure for each type of family law proceeding is the minimum standard for experienced family law attorneys. The most important step is identifying and understanding what influences and convinces each attorney and judge your family law attorney faces in your case. Strategic negotiation can happen only when your family law attorney knows your opponent.

Accounting is a substantial aspect of any family law case involving property or money. Family law attorneys are tasked with creating and reviewing budgets, financial statements, marital balance sheets, child support computations, alimony calculations, cash flow projections, and more—

such tasks are more accounting-related than most lawyers are accustomed. Family law attorneys must review tax returns and evaluate the tax implications of decisions in your case. In divorces involving business or investment assets, they are called upon to audit these assets and provide concise advice to clients on the legal implications of these issues.

Communication is a critical element in the skill set of every great family law attorney. The attorney turned family lawyer has inherent skill in understanding people and what makes them tick. Family lawyers must evaluate the complex issues of each family law case, learn about their client and what matters most to them, and then explain the ins and outs of that client's specific legal issues in such a way that the client can *hear and understand their family law attorney*. Recognizing that hearing and understanding a client are two separate things is key.

Few areas of law practice are as complex yet rewarding as family law. Family lawyers are the gladiators of the human condition; however, we enjoy nothing more than removing our armor and celebrating a win with every client we have the honor to serve.

Finding the right gladiator for you begins with ensuring these four qualities are present. This book provides the knowledge to evaluate and identify the best attorney for your specific needs. In becoming more familiar with the issues in your case, you will be better equipped to select the lawyer who can achieve the best outcome for you within your budget.

Feeling Empowered

I hope this book helps you understand the law and process that lie ahead or that you are currently in the throes of in your case. Either way, this book is written by a family law practitioner dedicated to being a Fierce Advocate® for clients in every situation addressed on these pages.

This book is dedicated to you, those facing divorce, child custody, division of assets, or any of the many other challenges clients face in family law. It covers topics similar to those in books written for practicing family law attorneys; however, it is not full of cases and complex terms of art. Rather, it is intended to be read and understandable by all.

It also presents my perspective on many specific issues in family law, which you will not find anywhere outside the resources provided by my firm, Cannon & Associates. Consider this book your look into the head of an experienced attorney who has helped thousands of clients facing issues similar to those you are facing.

We welcome you to reach out with questions about the information in this book or otherwise in family law, and, if we are the right fit for your needs, to engage us as Your Fierce Advocates®.

SECTION 2: BEFORE FILING FOR DIVORCE

"John and his staff are a force to be reckoned with. They are the epitome of a force to be reckoned with. They take your case seriously and they mean it when they say they fiercely advocate for their clients I would highly recommend John Cannon and his law firm with all of your family legal needs."

Fritznie

Building a relationship is like establishing a business. Not all relationships survive. Sometimes, even the sweetest marriages can fail and lead to a divorce. However, if your marriage is heading this way, the least you can do is protect yourself in preparation for the stress. Knowing what to do and how to do it can significantly improve your overall experience, whether you are the one seeking a divorce or you know that your spouse's filing for divorce is imminent.

Evaluating divorce, or another similar option, in your marriage is emotionally taxing. During an emotional time in your life, it is easy to lose track of what is important and how to safeguard yourself. In this section, we help you understand how to prepare for the divorce process, as much as anyone can prepare for it. We give an overview of legal, financial, practical, and emotional issues that you'll want to consider and tangible steps you can take to protect yourself before filing for divorce.

What Is Pre-Divorce Planning

Pre-divorce planning is what the name implies: a plan you make before the divorce filing for life after the divorce is final.

Pre-divorce planning is not analogous to vengeful or spiteful action. Preparation is not about taking your spouse for all they are worth or intentionally causing them pain during the process. You will *not* benefit from the following information if you want to hurt your spouse. Rather, pre-divorce planning is about preparing yourself for a mentally, emotionally, and likely physically difficult time in your life and organizing the complex process you are about to face in your divorce.

Whether you are the husband or wife, preparing yourself practically, financially, and emotionally, before divorce is essential to protect your future and potentially your children, especially if there are minor children from the marriage.

Questions in Pre-Divorce Planning?

Preparation is key to success in almost every endeavor, and this maxim also holds true for divorce. No marriage, nor any divorce, is identical. You and your chosen divorce attorney will not know how your divorce case will proceed until it is happening. However, by thinking through unique variables in your case, for example, your spouse, your finances, and the circumstances leading to divorce, you will be better prepared to identify potential problems in your divorce and possibly minimize or avoid them.

In addition to the steps to a pre-divorce plan outlined in this section of the book, you should consider all the following potential issues that are applicable to you:

- Where do you want to live after you are divorced?
- Do you want to keep the marital home after divorce?
- Do you want to buy a new home after divorce?
- Divorce can be expensive; do you have the funds ready for a divorce?
- During the divorce, will you have resources for living expenses?
- What support alimony will you need during divorce?
- What support alimony are you willing or able to pay during divorce?
- Do you want your children to live with you full-time after divorce?
- What custody plan or visitation schedule will work for you?
- After divorce, how do you want to divide bank accounts?
- Do you want to keep all of your retirement after divorce?
- Do you have the means to buy out your spouse's interest from an account they are entitled to a share of from the marriage?

Although this list brings up questions and issues we could spend pages discussing, they are not all important or applicable to you. Therefore, it is wise to sit down and jot out your questions or concerns about the divorce process before meeting with an experienced divorce attorney.

Legal Steps to Take Before Filing for Divorce

Although it involves many financial, practical, and emotional adjustments, divorce is at heart a legal process. You transition from legally married to legally divorced. It is, therefore, important to understand various legal issues before embarking on this transition.

Research Divorce Requirements

Typically, before someone files for divorce, they have considered the decision's repercussions for months or even years and want the process to be over quickly. Unfortunately, obtaining a final divorce takes much longer than most couples desire.

Many assume the divorce timeline is determined by the judge presiding over the case. However, most states have legal waiting periods and residency requirements that parties must meet before obtaining a divorce. The date you or your spouse files for divorce also starts the clock for when your divorce may be finalized. In most states, there is a minimum waiting period between the date you file for divorce and the date a divorce may be granted or finalized.

For example, a divorce without minor children in Oklahoma may be finalized within ten (10) days. However, a divorce with minor children cannot be finalized until ninety days have passed. These waiting periods add to the time it takes to finalize the divorce process and move on with your life.

In addition to the statutory waiting period, each state has other requirements to obtain a divorce. You or your spouse must prove your residency within the state for the divorce court to have jurisdiction to grant your divorce. For example, in Oklahoma, you or your spouse must have established residency in Oklahoma for at least six months and in the county of filing for thirty days for the court to have jurisdiction to hear your case.

In a divorce involving minor children, you may be required to complete a parenting seminar during the divorce process. For example, in Oklahoma, both parties in a divorce involving minor children must complete a parenting seminar.

Consider Custody

Divorce is difficult when it only involves two parties; however, it is even more challenging when children and custody are involved. When parents dispute custody and visitation in divorce, it can lead to a lengthy and expensive divorce. Additionally, many people incorrectly assume that mothers have a leg up in custody proceedings; however, this is no longer the case in most divorce courts.

Family law courts are tasked to evaluate children's best interest when deciding custody disputes. State family law courts do not automatically favor mothers in custody determinations. Many family law courts favor joint or shared custody arrangements; however, some family dynamics are not well suited for joint custody. In the early phases of considering divorce and child custody, you must consider your family's dynamics and what is best for your children. You may be able to create a custody plan, which you can present to your spouse early in the divorce process to minimize fighting over custody. Identifying the custody plans that may work for your family assists you in planning custody and other aspects of your divorce.

Adjust Legal Documents

Upon entry of a final Decree of Divorce, your assets may be protected from passing your former spouse; however, you should still consult with an estate planning attorney and at least consider entering new estate planning documents, such as a Will, Trust, and/or Life Insurance policy, if you have them, before filing for divorce. Additionally, if you do not have an advanced healthcare directive or your spouse has authority under your current plan, you should change this designation to another person you trust with this decision-making authority. It may be a complex process to disinherit your spouse; therefore, it is wise to consult with an estate planning attorney before making any changes that may or may not be enforceable.

Interview Divorce Attorneys Before You Need One

Meeting with and evaluating experienced divorce attorneys before deciding to file for divorce and before your spouse has filed gives you an advantage in considering options and potential issues in your divorce case. Even if you are in the initial stage of considering your options, including whether to file for divorce, an experienced family law attorney can advise you of your options and the best course of action for your circumstance. The best course of action for you at any given stage differs from someone else facing or considering divorce.

An experienced family law attorney can advise you on the law and procedures applicable to your specific concerns or questions related to divorce. Whether you want to obtain alimony, minimize your potential liability for alimony, obtain full custody or specific visitation with your children, or various other issues that are common or less common in divorce cases, an experienced family law attorney can answer your questions and give you a forecast of potential outcomes for your specific concern.

Whether you decide to seek divorce or another course of action, you benefit from contacting an experienced family law attorney to discuss your pain points and concerns for your potential divorce case. An experienced divorce attorney can explain the laws and rules applicable to your case and help you identify a strategy moving forward, whether you are ready to file for divorce or are only at the research stage.

Taking these actions will allow you to understand some of the main legal issues that might affect your divorce proceeding and be in a better position to protect your rights.

Financial Steps to Take Before Filing for Divorce

Divorce can be a financial shock. In addition to the costs of divorce proceedings, your access to income and assets may be negatively affected at the same time that you lose the ability to share living costs with your spouse. Not surprisingly, statistics reflect that women suffer financially after divorce more than men, as the average female's income reduces by almost 50% following divorce in the United States. Evaluating and protecting your financial situation before a divorce can help lessen the shock.

FINANCIALLY PREPARING FOR DIVORCE PROCEEDINGS During the divorce process, attorneys and courts may scrutinize your marital finances to determine issues like the appropriate division of assets (who gets what) as well as amounts of alimony or child support. Additionally, a lengthy proceeding can put stress on your personal financial situation. Here, we provide suggestions for preparing financially for the divorce process itself.

Categorize Assets and Debts

Upon divorce, all property held by either spouse is divided. How your property is divided between you and your spouse depends on state law. Unless a premarital agreement exists or your separate property has been maintained as separate property, your property will be split after your divorce.

For example, in Oklahoma, property that one spouse brings into the marriage that is "not comingled" may remain separate property. In contrast, property that was acquired before marriage but then blended with marital property or whose separate nature "cannot be traced" is potentially subject to marital division. For example, you will likely be able to keep a car you owned prior to marriage. Still, keeping a house you purchased before marriage may be more contested, even if a strong argument exists that the house is separate property.

Developing a marital balance sheet, a detailed list of marital versus separate property, and all identifiable debts, gives you a leg up in the divorce process. Clearly identifying all significant items of property and debts helps you consider the financial implications of divorce and assists an experienced divorce attorney in giving you the most accurate legal advice on the issue of property division in your divorce.

A well-documented marital balance sheet can significantly reduce the length of the discovery period and help you understand where you stand financially and what might be left after the divorce.

Organize Your Records

Time is money in divorce litigation, as your family law team will bill for anytime spent on your case. However, you can save yourself the grief and obtain clarity of the issues, assets, and debts in your divorce by obtaining and organizing a copy of all records before notifying your spouse that you are seeking a divorce. It is far easier to obtain financial records and other important records when you have access to the accounts used by your spouse and the marital home than after they are notified that you are seeking a divorce.

Gather all the documents that show the assets you brought into the marriage and all the gifts you received during the marriage. Make sure to document as much information as you remember, including secret debts, bank accounts, and assets.

In addition to financial records, you should take an inventory of valuable possessions, assets, and the amount of debt in all loans and credit cards for you and your spouse. Once you have gathered all the records of your household's finances, you may provide them to your financial advisor and divorce attorney for safekeeping. Technology is a great tool; so consider saving the records electronically in a location your spouse cannot access, such as a new Google Drive or Dropbox.

Save Proof of Income

Child support and alimony both consider the parties' incomes when calculating who pays and how much. This process is more complicated when you or your spouse have multiple income streams or own a business. All income, taxed or untaxed, payroll or profits, fixed or contingent, is subject to child support and alimony consideration, not including military disability and VA benefits.

Spouses are legally prohibited from hiding income and assets; however, this rule is difficult to enforce without private investigators and forensic accounting after a contentious divorce has begun. Therefore, if you are aware of varied income streams for your spouse, before filing for divorce, you need to act to obtain records of the varied sources of income. Income that is more diffuse than a paycheck is difficult to track. You can identify and maintain records over time. You can document your spouse's income using some of the following tools: email, texts, receipts, account deposits, contracts, and other relevant sources of information from his/her business.

Consider the Date of Separation

Upon the "date of separation," property and debt you acquire are separate and not subject to division. However, in the case of credit card debt, the division of responsibility to pay debts can be more confusing. By opening a separate credit card and discontinuing the use of all marital debts, you may more easily be able to claim you are not responsible for those debts, and they should be attributed to your spouse after the date of separation.

Either spouse's move out of the marital home may start the clock on your separation. In many states, the date a party moves out of the marital home, or even the marital bedroom, identifies the legal date of separation. In some states, like Oklahoma, the date of separation is not so simple because separation may be claimed when the parties have reached a state of no possible reconciliation and the marital bond has been destroyed. However, that is not so easy to identify.

The date you file for divorce is the last safe date to assume separation can be identified.

Take Enough Money Out of Your Joint Account

As part of the divorce process, joint accounts operated by the couple may be frozen. While this may not affect the personal accounts of each spouse, you should protect yourself by withdrawing half of your joint account.

When withdrawing money from the account, consider your welfare, attorney fees, and other responsibilities that may arise due to the intended legal separation. You must, however, be careful of the amount taken out. According to the state law, a spouse is allowed to take out as much as 50% from the joint account. You can get into hot water with the family law judge in the divorce action if you take more than 50% of the funds in any marital account.

Open New Accounts

Whether or not you decide to take money out of joint accounts or other accounts you can access, it is wise to secure enough funds to retain your chosen divorce attorney and sufficient funds to provide for your needs for the next few months. Identifying the funds you need during divorce is easier if you have developed a post-divorce budget, as we discuss below.

Opening a new checking, savings, and credit card account in your name only with the address of a new post office box (as we suggest below) gives you the security to begin building your separate financial future. These three financial tools give you financial independence since they are not impacted by your spouse's spending or their decision to limit your access to funds after learning about the divorce.

Create an Emergency Divorce Fund

Whether or not you are concerned that your spouse may try to freeze your access to marital funds, it is wise to establish an emergency divorce fund to cover your living expenses for six months, if possible. You will be well prepared for the divorce proceedings if you have saved money in a separate savings account. You will have a very difficult time hiring an experienced family lawyer if you do not have access to funds.

You may be susceptible to settling for less than you are entitled to or less than what is fair in your divorce case if you cannot pay your living expenses and are waiting for a divorce settlement's payout.

If you follow the above suggestions, you will be in a much stronger position to negotiate a fair and accurate division of assets, arrive at an appropriate alimony amount, and survive even a prolonged divorce without financial stress.

Financially Preparing for Life After Divorce

Knowing and managing your finances is one of the healthiest steps you can take to a new life during and after divorce. A good family law attorney aims to assist clients in not only affording a lifestyle they love after divorce but also improving financial health during and after divorce. It is important in marriage to develop a budget; however, it is even more important during and after divorce, due to new expenses and reduced income.

Financial wellness will always evade you if you do not plan; creating a budget is an important step in taking control of your financial health. During and after the divorce process, a budget can assist you in getting a grasp on your finances and learning to be a better money manager.

Financial health or financial wellness does not come from simply creating a budget. You need to identify your spending habits as well as look at the facts of your spending to create a healthy budget going forward.

Building a budget after divorce is a great start to better financial health and confidence in supporting yourself and your children after divorce. In this section, we provide suggestions for how to build a post-divorce budget.

Adopt the Right Attitude

The adage of "spend less than you make" is insufficient when seeking to protect yourself financially during and after divorce. You leave money on the table you could have accessed if you oversimplify the process of creating a post-divorce budget. By thinking through and developing a realistic budget, you will be better able to achieve your financial goals and feel confident in your ability to support yourself after divorce.

You will be much closer to financial freedom after divorce if you go beyond accepting that you can "afford your lifestyle now," as that may not be the case after the divorce is finalized. The suggestions here put you in a better position to make strategic decisions in your divorce case and about personal spending.

Evaluate Your Future Financial Prospects

It is obvious to most people that divorce has negative financial consequences. However, many parties fail to realize they must support themselves, their existing savings may be divided, and your income may be reduced drastically, while your expenses may stay relatively the same.

Many married parties do not realize that an obligation for spousal support beyond marriage is very common. Alimony or spousal support is awarded in many cases, even if it is temporary in almost all cases. It is unlikely that you will be required to pay or be provided spousal support beyond five years, but if you are required to pay, this expense is in addition to child support and the division of your property.

In some states, alimony may last much longer than anticipated and be greater than expected. Where longer-term spousal support is supported in law, the basic premise is that alimony is based on the dependent spouse's need for alimony and the other spouse's ability to pay spousal support. We will dive deeper into alimony in Section 6. Evaluating your future financial needs assists you in considering your options in divorce.

Create a Marital Income Statement

Do not be scared by the term "Marital Income Statement." In this context, I'm simply telling you to list your current income and expenses. You can begin by taking a sheet of paper, drawing a line down the middle, and listing all sources of income on one side and expenses on the other. Examples of the sources of income and expenses you should include are as follows:

Sources of Income	Expenses
• Salary	• Rent or Mortgage payments
• Bonuses	• Insurance
• Investments	• Vehicle Loan
• Social Security	• Credit Cards
• Support Alimony	• Utilities
• Child Support	• Food
• Retirement	• Vehicle Expenses
• Any other sources of income	• Any other monthly expenses

At this point, do not worry about identifying every single expense; you can refine your Marital Income Statement over time, which is why we recommend keeping the information in a computer file.

Hopefully, when you tally your expenses, they are less than your income. Either way, do not celebrate or panic yet. Knowledge is power, and the first step to creating financial health is identifying the facts and the problem if one exists.

You can increase your income if it is vital to do so. You could begin freelance work in your industry if it is not prohibited by your employer, sell property, or create a product to sell. However, if your expenses need to decrease drastically for financial independence after divorce, you can easily downsize your home or vehicle in most scenarios.

You must start somewhere on the road to financial health during and after divorce. Tracking your income and expenses is the first step to giving you a handle on your money and peace of mind with your finances after divorce.

Isolate Essential Expenses, Nothing Else

Once you have created a Marital Income Statement, including a detailed summary of your expenses, it is time to take a more critical look at them. You must first identify your essential expenses, not the expenses you enjoy, but what you *must* spend each month to support you and, if relevant, your children. Your essential expenses should include your rent or mortgage, any child support or alimony obligations, insurance, groceries (not your monthly tab for eating out), utilities, transportation, and only a few other expenses.

Your essential expenses do not include your gym membership, cable, Netflix, or Disney Plus account. By beginning with identifying the essential expenses to support yourself, you're developing a framework for understanding your spending habits and setting a course for financial security beyond divorce.

Identify Discretionary Expenses

After identifying your essential expenses during or after divorce, you can begin to identify and prioritize nonessential or discretionary expenses. Discretionary expenses are important to identify during divorce as they give you an easy option to reduce your expenditures or balance your monthly post-divorce budget. Some of the most common and expensive types of discretionary spending include eating out and entertainment. It's not that you should live without these things; however, if you pack your lunch four days a week and reduce your entertainment subscriptions, you will likely identify over $1,000 in savings each month.

Understanding your discretionary spending allows you to be strategic in reducing or cutting expenses to maintain financial security during the divorce process and beyond.

Understand your Net Income, Not Gross Income

Once you clearly understand your essential expenses and discretionary expenses, your attention should turn to developing a more thoughtful understanding of your income. Most people choose to believe if they make $5,000 a month, they have access to that total amount for spending. Most people fail to remember that taxes, payroll deductions, and social security are all taken out of your paycheck before you have access to these funds. Put simply, if your salary is $100,000, you do not have $100,000 to spend.

Knowing your net income, the funds you have access to each month, is essential to understanding your finances. If your net income is insufficient to cover your essential expenses, identifying a side business or additional employment can help increase your income. Whatever your income, your financial security during and after divorce improves with an acute understanding of your net income for purposes of your post-divorce budget.

Meet with a Professional

These post-divorce budget suggestions may sound simple here; however, it can be very complicated to identify and understand all the numbers that go into your post-divorce budget, or any budget. Professionals, such as tax advisors, financial planners, and CPAs, all exist to assist people with understanding their finances. You do not have to go it alone in identifying your divorce budget or post-divorce budget.

Develop Healthy Spending Habits

You can more easily track and adjust your essential and discretionary spending with a detailed understanding of your divorce budget. When you track where your money is spent each month, you can better identify spending habits and modify them for your financial peace of mind during and after your divorce. Shocking as it may be, one single adjustment to your spending may save you thousands of dollars over a year, which may be all it takes to give you financial security after divorce.

You will be in a far better position than most if you follow through with the first six steps to creating a healthy post-divorce budget. Simply knowing what you can and can't afford gives you more financial peace of mind than most individuals facing divorce, or recently divorced.

Establish Credit in Your Name or Increase Your Existing Score

Once your divorce is final, it will be important to have credit in your name or as high a credit score as possible to assist with renting an apartment, qualifying for the best mortgage options for a new home, obtaining a car loan, and receiving a credit card with an attractive interest rate in your name. You can now act to establish credit in your own name if you have never done so. You can begin by researching credit card companies to determine what options and benefits are best for the new you after divorce.

In some circumstances, if your spouse has established credit, it can be transferred to you; however, it is always safer to begin by requesting a free credit score report on yourself from one of the three major providers: Experian, Equifax, or Credit Karma. Once you obtain your credit score, you will know more about your ability to get credit. Obtaining a credit card in your name, consistently paying, and completing other steps may increase your credit score before you need it. Regardless of your credit status, increasing your credit score makes life easier after divorce, at least financially.

The above suggestions will allow you to enjoy greater financial stability and independence after your divorce is finalized than if you avoid such planning.

Practical Steps to Take Before Filing for Divorce

You may need to take specific personal organization steps or adjust your personal life to prepare for divorce and its aftermath.

Make Other Plans for Your Welfare

Certain things can complicate your divorce. Impregnating your partner during the process, among other things, can nullify the chances of a simple result in divorce. You may need to start making other plans for your accommodation and welfare to protect yourself and the case. Be sure to plan carefully where to live and how to go about your life as normally as possible until the case has been finalized. It is wise to set up new routines and habits that help take your focus off your pending divorce and focus on your future and relationship with your family and children separate from your spouse.

Rent a Post Office Box

You need to identify an address where you can receive mail, so it cannot be intercepted or tampered with by your spouse. Renting a post office box from the nearest US Post Office is the easiest way to establish an address your spouse cannot access. You may want to receive information in the mail before your spouse knows that you are filing for divorce, and a separate address is the only way to ensure that they do not receive mail you do not want them to see.

Additionally, a separate address inaccessible to your spouse gives you peace of mind that your new credit card or bank account information, correspondence with your divorce attorney, and other paperwork you want to remain private can do so.

Open a New Email Account

Most married people have had access to their spouse's email account at one time or another. Even if you believe your spouse cannot access your email account, it is wise to assume they can read everything in your email. In our technological age, it is safe to assume much of your private information, including your divorce information, will be in your email account. Therefore, it is wise to open a new email account with a separate provider than your primary account. Open a Google Gmail account if you use Yahoo, or the reverse. You can have peace of mind that correspondence between you and your attorney will not be visible to your spouse if they do not know about the new account that you are communicating sensitive information on.

Social Media During Divorce

The topic of social media and divorce could fill up an entire book, but for the purposes here, be careful with your social media accounts. You should never discuss your divorce or spouse on social media as the content is easily accessible and never destroyed. Additionally, you should change the password to all social media and other internet-accessible accounts. Your spouse is not entitled to access this information, but there is no time that a spouse would be more motivated to access your social media accounts and violate your trust than when you are facing divorce.

The best advice is to completely avoid social media during your divorce and change the password to something your spouse cannot guess. However, if you must tweet, Snapchat, or get on TikTok or Facebook, do so with discretion and change your passwords! You can reduce stress and increase your preparedness for your divorce case by following the essential steps in your pre-divorce planning discussed above.

Emotional and Mental Health Steps to Take Before Filing for Divorce

Create an Emotional and Financial Support Structure for Yourself

It's hard to see a relationship one has invested in for years evaporate. The emotional effect can be crushing. During this period, you should create a support structure of friends, family, and healthy habits. In addition, you should put a financial support structure in place to see you through the legal process. Emotional support can and likely should include seeking a divorce therapist or divorce counselor during the process, as we suggest next.

Consider Your Mental Health

Divorce is emotionally and mentally exhausting for most people. No one got married expecting to seek one day to end the marriage. However, divorce is the best thing for some marriages due to several factors. The most important thing to do during the process is to protect your children and your mental health. You may want to get through the process as quickly as possible if you are determined to file for divorce. However, you should not give up on important issues or property simply to reach a conclusion.

The process will end at some point, and in many instances, both your financial future and your children's future will benefit from your taking the time to ensure you maximize the outcome of your case. We recommend anyone considering divorce seek help, including counseling to deal with the difficult emotions that accompany divorce.

Mental health professionals, especially a psychiatrist or counselor with training in grief counseling or divorce counseling, may be a great resource to help you and/or your children with the pains of divorce. Do not consider yourself weak for seeking counseling during the process. It is a sign of strength to first identify you need help and then obtain the right kind of help. Do not forsake the mental health of your children or yourself during the divorce process. Our team at Cannon & Associates is passionate about helping every client reach their **Better Future Now**, which includes seeking mental health services for many of our clients.

Wait on Building a New Relationship

Most people desire companionship and love, which is a major reason many are drawn to new relationships during divorce. Dating during separation can reduce your motivation to complete the process and negatively impact your children if they learn about your new romantic interest.

In a no-fault state, you do not have to prove the other party is at fault to obtain a divorce, and the other party cannot use your misconduct against you in court. The last statement comes with the following caveat: if your conduct has the potential to negatively impact your children or unjustly enrich you, the court may consider that conduct when evaluating property division and custody. For example, suppose you have been the primary earner in your home and you have a new love interest. In that case, your argument for an inability to pay alimony weakens if you have a love interest that you are spending money on in lieu of paying alimony.

In fault-based divorce states, an extramarital relationship during a divorce can negatively impact you in the divorce process, especially financially. Whether you are in a fault-based divorce state or no-fault divorce state, we advise you to hold off on a new romantic relationship during the divorce or before the divorce process is finalized, for you personally, for your children, and strategically for your divorce case as well.

Talk to Your Spouse

Few things in life are less comfortable than telling your spouse that you are filing for divorce. However, they likely suspected the conversation was coming eventually if it had come to that point. It takes two people to get a divorce, and it is often safe to say the other party was aware of your decision before your telling them that you were filing for divorce.

Although uncomfortable, your chances of an amicable or collaborative divorce are greatly increased if you communicate to your spouse about your decision and desired outcome. A caveat to this advice: if you have a toxic marriage, are in danger of domestic abuse, or are concerned your spouse may use information you provide against you, then you should leave it to your chosen divorce attorney and the family law firm you have hired to communicate that you are seeking a divorce.

However, if safe and sensible to attempt a collaborative divorce, you have a higher likelihood of a smoother process, expending less on attorney fees, and suffering less emotionally than during a contested divorce.

SECTION 3: DIVORCE 101

"Very professional and truly cares for his clients. Delivers peace of mind while quickly working in your behalf. Would strongly recommend to anyone going through a difficult situation!! Thank you Cannon & Associates for all you've done and continue doing for me and my family."

Cody

Divorce is commonly considered one of the most difficult experiences a person goes through. Although a divorce case is basically the same as any civil case, the stakes involved are far higher than those in a routine lawsuit since the outcome will affect your home, your children, your property, and much more. Understanding how divorce cases work and the various issues at stake beyond the legal dissolution of your marriage can help you navigate the process and defend your rights, property, and relationship with your children during your divorce case.

In this section, we explain the divorce process generally and help you understand related family law matters that might arise in your case, such as child custody and support and alimony. We also explain some factors that might make the process smoother, such as having a prenuptial agreement or being able to agree to an uncontested divorce, or more difficult, such as seeking a protective order or paternity disputes. This section is a high-level overview; we go into more detail about specific issues later in this book.

The Basics of the Divorce Process

Oklahoma Divorce Process

Petition for Divorce
Legal Document initiating Oklahoma divorce, which is filed with the Court Clerk in your County.

Petition Served on Spouse
Petition, Summons, and Application for Temporary Orders, if filed, served on Respondent; thus initiating Divorce Proceeding.

Spouse's Response Due
Respondent must file a Response within 30 days of being served with Petition. He/She must respond to every claim and assert his/her own defenses and allegations.

Temporary Orders
This is a vital step in your divorce to establish the temporary plan for custody, residence, alimony, debts, and other issues. Often temporary orders are close to the final orders.

Discovery in Divorce
Tool to ensure you gather critical information and evidence related to assets, claims, and defenses. The four most common tools include: Interrogatories, Requests for Production, Admissions, and Depositions

Mediation
Neutral third party, typically an experienced attorney, facilitates discussion between the parties in an effort to reach an agreement without the expense/uncertainty of trial.

Settlement Discussions
Many cases settle shortly before or after mediation. We can assist you in seeking the outcome you desire in your case without trial.

Going to Trial
Your divorce trial will likely be six months to a year after your petition is filed. The Court will make a final decision in all unresolved aspects of your divorce.

CANNON
& ASSOCIATES

Settlement Agreement
Divorce Finalized

Filing a Petition & Summons

A divorce is started by one party, the "Petitioner" filing a "Petition for Dissolution of Marriage." If you are the one filing the Petition, it is your opportunity to notify the court of the outcome you want regarding all the issues that must be resolved in a divorce. The filing of a Petition for

Dissolution of Marriage initiates the divorce proceeding. The Petition must include information about the parties seeking divorce; the jurisdiction of the court to hear the case; and typically includes the Petitioner's proposal for settling the issues in the case, including custody, property division, alimony, child support, debt allocation, retirement, and other issues.

The Summons in a divorce action is the formal notice that the Petitioner has initiated the case. The Summons notifies the other party, the Respondent, that they must file an Answer within a set number of days (twenty days in Oklahoma) of the Petition, or they risk giving up rights in the case. The court may issue a default judgment, a judgment in favor of one party because the other party has failed to act. The summons must be served on the Respondent unless they waive service by summons.

Automatic Temporary Injunctions & Orders

The "Petition" is often filed with an "Application for Temporary Orders," which is the Petitioner's request for orders from the Court that will remain in place until the divorce is finalized. Divorce cases can take considerable time, especially when children are involved. Frequently, it is in one or both parties' best interest to set ground rules. The Temporary Orders covers child custody, child visitation, child support, possession of the marital home, possession of vehicles, support alimony, possession of specific assets, and sets the proper conduct of the parties during the divorce process.

The Temporary Orders are, in addition to Automatic Temporary Injunctions (ATIN), put in place by the court, which stop both parties from selling, transferring, or reducing assets of the parties, increasing the mutual debt of the parties, removing a party from insurance, or other damaging acts.

Response/Answer & Counter-Petition

Once the Respondent (the spouse who did not file the case) has been served, they must file an Answer stating their position on each claim or allegation in the Petition. Additionally, the Respondent may file a Counter-Petition stating his/her claims in the case.

In divorces where both parties agree on the terms of divorce or the parties are not very contentious, your chosen attorney can handle all the necessary legal paperwork to complete what is called an uncontested or "waiver" divorce. This is because the Respondent is waiving their rights and accepting the divorce. The parties can enter a Settlement Agreement and work towards a Decree for Dissolution of Marriage, or "Divorce Decree," if they agree on all the divorce terms. If the parties can agree to some but not all terms, they can enter a "Stipulated Order." However, it is still in your interest to file a Response and Counterclaim for Temporary Orders, if the Petition filed them.

However, in divorces where the parties cannot agree on terms, the case proceeds with hearings, discovery, and eventually trial if the parties do not resolve their divorce at mediation.

Motion Practice

Motions in any family law case are simply a request by one or both parties for specific orders of the court during the pendency of the case. Either party may submit a formal request to the family law judge for orders during the divorce. Some of the most common motions involve requests for protective orders, restraining orders, motions to compel discovery (meaning giving information to the other party, as discussed below), motions to enforce existing court orders, and motions to modify current court orders.

Hearings

Some issues during a family law case cannot be resolved by the agreement of the parties. In addition to reviewing and deciding on the written motions described above, sometimes the court must hold a hearing to decide the outcome of issues in a family law case before the case goes to trial. For example, a common issue litigated in contested divorce cases is where children live during the divorce.

Both parties may fight to have physical custody of their children during the divorce by filing an Application for Temporary Orders and holding a hearing before the family law judge. After the hearing, the judge issues temporary orders, which can or will be changed in the final divorce decree or child custody order.

Discovery

Discovery in a family law case, similar to other types of civil cases, is the process that allows each party to submit requests to the other for information, admissions, or documents, which, in theory, allows both parties to learn more about the opposing party's case and position. The primary tools in discovery are interrogatories (questions to the other party), requests for admissions, requests for production (documents and other tangible evidence), and depositions (questioning the other party under oath). Often, the information or documents obtained through the discovery process are of great importance for learning the strengths and weaknesses in the opposing party's case.

Mediation

Family law judges frequently require the parties to participate in nonbinding mediation prior to a contested divorce or child custody trial. Mediation is a process in which both parties present their side of the case, including custody, assets, finances, and every other issue, to a neutral third-party mediator (usually an attorney), who advises on what they think is reasonable or what the trial judge would likely order. Being properly prepared for this step in the process often allows you and your divorce attorney resolve your divorce without trial if the parties reach an agreement during mediation.

Trial & Judgement

At trial, the terms of the divorce are no longer entirely within the parties' control, rather a judge decides the terms of the divorce, including child custody, child visitation, support orders, division of assets and debts, and other issues.

Divorce or child custody trials are the final hearing before the original divorce court. Both parties present evidence, witnesses, financial records, and even expert witnesses in some cases. The family law judge listens to both parties and decides the outcome of all issues before the court. The court's final orders, whether agreed or decided at a contested divorce trial, govern child custody, child support, division of the marital assets, spousal support, and all other issues in a divorce or child custody case.

The decisions at trial are enforced upon the parties. If an issue is decided in a way you dislike or find unsatisfactory, you have the right to appeal the judge's decision; however, there is no guarantee you will like the result from the appellate review either. If no appeal is filed, the parties must draft the necessary documents to enforce the court's judgment.

"Shortcuts" in the Divorce Process

As we explained in *The Basics of the Divorce Process*, several procedural steps exist to obtain a final divorce order. If you have a prenuptial agreement, or you can work out an uncontested divorce, you will be able to avoid some of these steps or some of the disputes that often make the divorce process so protracted and stressful.

Prenuptial Agreements

A Pre-Nuptial Agreement can speed up the divorce process by avoiding lengthy disputes about financial matters.

Often one person has substantially greater assets than their soon-to-be spouse and desires to protect these interests in case the future marriage does not work out. The best way to do so is by entering a mutually agreed upon prenuptial agreement before you say, "I do." Prenuptial agreements are valid in most states.

Entering a prenuptial agreement does not mean you do not trust your future spouse, rather, it is a way for both sides to protect their separate interests and state they are marrying for love, not financial gain. Even where one future spouse is wealthier than the other, both parties to a prenuptial agreement have interests that can be protected or memorialized in the agreement, such as agreeing that a percentage of the estate or assets be transferred to one spouse if infidelity occurs, which can also result in terminating the marriage.

If you are already married and do not already have a prenuptial agreement, the information in this section, while interesting, may not be helpful to you.

What Is a Prenuptial Agreement?

On its most basic level, a prenuptial agreement is as simple as it sounds: an agreement or contract before "nuptial" (marriage) between the parties to be married. Prenuptial agreements determine the sharing of finances during marriage and the division of assets and accounts upon divorce.

State law typically allows parties to contract almost anything as long as it is not unconscionable or unacceptable on its face. However, state law may impose certain requirements for establishing an enforceable prenuptial agreement due to the potential for divesting one party of their marital share or interest in assets, income, or property.

What Is Required for a Valid Prenuptial Agreement?

Because prenuptial agreements are similar to contracts, state laws require the parties to respect certain requirements for the prenuptial agreement to be valid. Some states require the prenuptial agreement to be in writing and signed by both parties. Additionally, courts have required that neither party be under fraud, duress, or coercion when agreeing to the prenuptial agreement for it to be valid.

Are Prenuptial Agreements Enforceable?

When there is a dispute, courts have routinely enforced prenuptial agreements if the agreement accurately reflects the desired financial agreement between the parties before entering marriage. For example, in Oklahoma, courts analyze prenuptial agreements as contracts: contracts are interpreted "to give effect to the mutual intention of the parties, as it existed at the time of contracting. The rule applies to prenuptial agreements."[1]

---

[1] Francis v. Francis, 285 P. 3d 707 (2012).

Additionally, state law often extends the effect of the written prenuptial agreement to be enforceable against any conflicting provisions of a deceased spouse's will. Courts have routinely enforced prenuptial agreements against the objecting spouse and other family trying to alter the original financial agreement of the parties.

Are Prenuptial Agreements Signed Immediately Before the Wedding Considered Valid?

Yes, as long as both parties fully understand the contract and its terms, it will be valid. There is no hard rule about the timing for signing a prenuptial agreement; however, it is best practice to sign the contract weeks or months before the wedding to ensure there is no undue pressure.

What Are the Benefits of a Prenuptial Agreement?

Prenuptial agreements allow the future spouses to:

- Clearly define each individual's finances and the marriage's collective finances.
- Creates a fair financial agreement for both parties.
- Enjoy peace of mind that the marriage is for love, not financial gain.
- Define how financial gains after the date of marriage are handled if the marriage ends in divorce.
- Clarify much of the uncertainty surrounding financial matters if the marriage ends in divorce.

These last two points are why prenuptial agreements represent a potential shortcut in divorce.

What Is a Prenuptial Agreement Unable to Do?

Prenuptial agreements do not allow the future spouses to:

- Determine the manner you raise your children or make decisions during the marriage.
- Establish the roles each spouse will hold in the marriage.
- Pre-determine child custody or child support if the marriage ends in divorce.

Consequently, having a prenuptial agreement may not speed up the divorce process if the couple has significant disputes about their children.

How Do I Get a Prenuptial Agreement?

If you are not yet married, you should discuss your desires concerning a prenuptial agreement with your fiancé before seeking advice from an attorney. Specifically, you need to discuss how finances, assets, and accounts are to be divided or distributed upon divorce or the death of one party. Both parties should seek separate attorneys to assist in the formation of your prenuptial agreement to ensure it complies with the substantive and procedural requirements of state law governing prenuptial agreements.

If you have a prenuptial agreement in place and are considering or already involved in a divorce case, you should ensure that the family law attorney you hire is experienced in the enforcement of prenuptial agreements.

Uncontested Divorce

Divorce or dissolution of marriage is never an easy experience for those involved. Most divorces are litigious, meaning the parties fight over some, or many, issues with the assistance of their divorce attorneys. However, uncontested divorce is a process that allows the parties to avoid the norm of fighting in divorce with a much shorter time frame for resolving issues and finalizing the divorce. In other words, an uncontested divorce is faster, less costly and less stressful than the average divorce.

This section explains the uncontested divorce process, highlighting the main differences between the contested and uncontested divorce.

What Is an Uncontested Divorce?

An uncontested divorce is somewhat self-explanatory. The parties agree on the division of real property, division of personal property, division of debts, child custody, child support, spousal support, and other issues commonly litigated in a contested divorce. Even if you and your spouse reach an agreement on every issue in your divorce and you want to pursue an uncontested divorce, it is in your best interest to work with an experienced divorce attorney to ensure your rights and interests are protected in the divorce decree and other divorce orders and that you are prepared in case your uncontested divorce develops into something more complicated. Reaching an agreement with your spouse on these issues can, however, provide the opportunity to save significantly on fees paid to your divorce attorney as compared to a contested divorce.

What Is the Process of an Uncontested Divorce?

The following is a snapshot of the necessary steps to complete an uncontested divorce. We strongly recommend speaking with and retaining an experienced divorce attorney to assist you through the waiver divorce process.

1. PETITION FOR DISSOLUTION OF MARRIAGE

As with the standard divorce process, a party initiates the uncontested divorce action by filing a Petition for divorce or dissolution of marriage. One difference from the normal process is that in an uncontested divorce, the parties can submit to the court jointly, or one party can present the documents alone. You will be forced to go through the contested divorce process if you and your spouse are unable to reach an agreement on every issue in your divorce; the divorce must be truly uncontested. Additionally, in some states, you can only seek a waiver or uncontested divorce if you file a no-fault divorce action.

2. WAIVER OF SUMMONS AND RIGHT TO ANSWER

In a waiver divorce, if the parties did not file jointly, the Respondent (meaning the spouse who did not file the Petition for divorce) waives service of process, giving up the right to receive proper notice that they have been sued for divorce. In an uncontested divorce, the Respondent may waive the service of process notification by signing and returning the waiver of summons pleading to the Petitioner's divorce attorney. The Petitioner's divorce attorney files the signed waiver of summons in the court where the uncontested divorce is filed, notifying the court that service of the Petition is no longer necessary.

The Respondent in an uncontested divorce also "waives" or gives up the right to file an Answer or Counter-Petition for Dissolution of Marriage. An Answer or Counter-Petition is not necessary in a waiver or uncontested divorce, if the Respondent agrees with the Petitioner's proposed Decree of Divorce. the proposed Decree of Divorce should lay out the agreement of both parties for the division of property, debts, child custody, child support, and all other issues necessary to complete an uncontested divorce.

3. CONTENTS OF DECREE OF DISSOLUTION OF MARRIAGE

The decree of dissolution of marriage or divorce decree is similar to the petition for dissolution of marriage; however, it is framed as orders of the court, as opposed to requests or "Petitions" to the court. A divorce decree has multiple requirements in order to be legally sufficient and to protect your interests and the interests of your spouse. The family law judge in your case does not give you legal advice or assist you in ensuring that your divorce decree is legally sufficient to be enforceable or protect your interests. This is one of the many reasons it is imperative to retain an experienced divorce attorney, even in an agreed waiver divorce.

This section does not cover the specifics of every legal requirement to create a legally sufficient and enforceable divorce decree; however, the following elements are essential for inclusion in your divorce decree:

Division of Property and Spousal Support Issues

The following are required in any divorce decree:

- Identification and division of all separate property (non-marital property)
- Division of all marital debts
- Identification and division of all individual debts
- Terms of spousal support (alimony) or the absence of spousal support

Child Custody and Child Support Issues

The following are also required if there are minor children in the divorce

- Legal custody determination: i.e. Custody Plan
- Physical custody schedule
- Holiday visitation schedule / summer visitation schedule
- Child support schedule and obligation

4. PREPARING DECREE OF DISSOLUTION OF MARRIAGE

You cannot simply file a divorce decree in an uncontested divorce. Instead, you must ensure all the following requirements are met before appearing for a hearing on your uncontested divorce before a family law judge. The necessary elements must be included in the divorce decree:

- Both parties must sign the divorce decree and all essential pleadings.
- In some instances, a jurisdictional affidavit is necessary for divorce that supports the Court's authority over the parties.

Once all the pleadings and documents are finalized, you can schedule a hearing before the family law judge assigned to your case (as automatically assigned in counties with more than one judge that handles the domestic/family docket, which is an operation within the court clerk's office), and you or your divorce attorney must appear to present your waiver divorce to the family law judge.

5. HEARING ON WAIVER DIVORCE

After you file the petition for divorce and the waiver of summons, before a Notary Public, and entry of appearance by your spouse, you and your divorce attorney may schedule a hearing before the assigned family law judge to finalize your divorce. In many states, there is a mandatory waiting period (for example, ten days in Oklahoma) before appearing before the family law judge to finalize your divorce. The waiting period may be significantly longer if minor children are involved.

For example, Oklahoma family law requires a ninety-day waiting period before finalizing a divorce involving minor children. Additionally, in some jurisdictions, the family law judge requires both parents to complete a parenting class on the impact of divorce on children before finalizing their divorce.

Even with these requirements and waiting periods, an uncontested divorce provides a much faster alternative to the standard (or contested) divorce described earlier in *The Basics of the Divorce Process.*

Additional Steps: When an Uncontested Divorce Becomes Contested

Most divorcing spouses who decide to attempt or enter the uncontested divorce process plan to resolve their divorce without issues or contention. However, issues or disputes can arise that make presenting a mutually agreed divorce decree impossible. When an uncontested divorce becomes contested, it is important to have an experienced Oklahoma divorce attorney on your side to present your case and protect your interests. The following are some of the most common additional steps that become necessary when an uncontested divorce becomes a contested divorce:

1. MEDIATION

Divorce mediation is a powerful tool to help resolve semi-contested divorces. In divorce mediation, both parties appear with their divorce attorney if they have retained counsel and present their case and petition to a divorce mediator. Skilled divorce mediators are, typically, family law attorneys or divorce attorneys with years of experience litigating divorce cases. Divorce mediators use their experience to forecast potential outcomes in a divorce trial or litigation and help the parties reach a mutually agreeable resolution of all the issues in their divorce. Mediators in divorce act as an unbiased, neutral third parties who facilitate open discussion between the parties while adding insight from years of experience.

The mediation process may take half a day or an entire day; however, it is less expensive and far less stressful than a contested family law trial in open court where anyone may watch and listen, including your family or adult children. Additionally, most family law judges require mediation before scheduling a divorce trial.

2. COLLABORATIVE DIVORCE

Collaborative divorce, unlike mediation, involves only the parties and their counsel; there is no neutral third party. Instead, the parties and their divorce attorneys strive to communicate and reach a settlement that is mutually beneficial and fair to the parties. The goal of collaborative divorce is the same as mediation: a fair and efficient resolution to divorce. Unlike in a contested divorce, in collaborative divorce, the parties' respective divorce attorneys act less as advocates for their clients and focus more on what is best for the family as a whole.

Every divorce is difficult and emotionally taxing; however, an uncontested divorce can minimize the negative impacts on you and your family. An uncontested divorce can save time and money, particularly if you retain an experienced divorce attorney to help streamline your divorce and ensure your rights and interests are protected while avoiding costly litigation.

In an uncontested divorce, you may be able to avoid ever appearing in person before the family law judge or simply appear once to present your waiver divorce/uncontested divorce to the judge, as opposed to a contested divorce in which you may appear multiple times for contested hearings before the judge.

Additionally, an uncontested divorce is likely to lead to a more amicable relationship between former spouses after divorce. This is partly because an uncontested divorce filed as a no-fault divorce allows the parties to complete their divorce without bringing years of pain and baggage into the equation.

"Speed Bumps" in the Divorce Process

In *The Basics of the Divorce Process*, we described the process of obtaining a final divorce order. As complicated as it is, this process can be even more difficult when child custody is at issue, paternity is in dispute, or an order of protection is requested.

This section presents an overview of these challenges. We provide more detail about each later in this book.

Child Custody

Often in a divorce case or a legal separation, parents battle over custody of their children and the terms of their upbringing after divorce. However, absent a custody order from a court, both parents are entitled to physical custody of any child born during the marriage or any child born to the parents before marriage where there is a mutual agreement that the husband is the child's father.

What Does Child Custody Mean?

Child custody includes both physical custody and legal custody. Physical custody determines where and with whom each child will live after the divorce. Legal custody, on the other hand, refers to a parent's right to make long-term decisions about raising the children. For example, a parent with legal custody makes decisions regarding a child's education and medical care.

A court can award sole custody or joint custody. Sole custody exists when only one parent has the right to make decisions regarding where a child will live (physical custody) or decisions about raising the child (legal custody). Physical custody describes where the child or children sleep at night, i.e. primary physical custody or visitation.

How Do I Get a Custody Order from the Court?

To get a custody order from the court, either parent must file a Petition for Custody. Once the Petition has been filed, the court must decide whether it has authority, or "jurisdiction," to determine custody of the child. Jurisdiction is typically based on where the child resides and how long they have lived there. For example, courts have jurisdiction in Oklahoma if the child has resided in Oklahoma for the past six months. When a child has lived outside of Oklahoma for at least six months, Oklahoma courts might decide another state is more appropriate to determine custody.

A court may issue a Temporary Custody Order, which involves a physical and legal custody agreement between the parents or an Order by the court that is legally binding until a final order from the court has been entered. A Temporary Order is often entered within the first 60 days after filing your divorce or custody action and may usually set parameters to be enforced after the case is finalized; so essentially, Temporary Orders may be very close to the final orders in your case. Although a court's final order *may* differ from the agreements made in the Temporary Order, the final order often doesn't differ. It is very important to have experienced counsel assist in preparing and presenting your case for Temporary Orders.

How Does a Court Decide Which Parent to Award Physical Custody?

Courts and experienced family law and child custody attorneys will tell you "the best interest of the child" determines child custody. State family law statutes detail what the court is to consider. The primary question examined by the court is what is in "the best interests of the physical, mental and moral welfare of the child."

For example, in Oklahoma, judges consider the following factors in custody matters:

- The wishes of each parent and the wishes of the child (depending on the child's age);
- The quality of the relationship between the child and each parent;
- The child's relationship with grandparents, siblings, and other significant people in the child's life;
- The child's relationship to their school, religious institutions, and community;
- The mental and physical health of all parties;
- Any past or present drug or substance abuse by either parent;
- Any past or present criminal actions by either parent (other than minor infractions or offenses that were committed a long time ago);
- Each parent's past involvement in getting the child to medical appointments;
- Each parent's involvement in the child's schooling;
- Each parent's ability to provide a safe home environment;
- The willingness of each parent to help foster a relationship and visitation with the other parent;
- Each parent's ability to provide a stable home life;
- Each parent's ability to provide for the child's material needs;
- Each parent's ability to spend time with the child.

The parent not awarded primary physical custody is often awarded certain visitation privileges. The court can order different types of visitations based on what is "in the best interest of the child."

Weekend visitation involves visits over a weekend from a set time on Friday until a set time on either Sunday night or Monday morning. Holiday visitation involves a schedule that alternates between certain holidays, including birthday visitation, Father's Day and Mother's Day visitation, Christmas visitation, Thanksgiving visitation, fall break visitation, summer break visitation, and spring break visitation. These holiday visitation periods provide some certainty of time the non-custodial parent has with the children. Your child custody attorney can explain the process and implication of the custody award.

Can I Change a Final Custody Order?

You can seek to change the final custody orders in your case. To request the court change the final orders, you must file a "Motion to Modify Custody Order." Generally, your motion should be filed in the same court and in the same case that issued the original order. When you file such a motion, you have to provide a reason that a change in the custody order is necessary. The standard to change custody orders differs depending on whether the order is a "sole custody order" or a "joint custody order." We provide more detail about each of these standards later in this book. In any event, you should speak to an experienced child custody attorney before filing a Motion to Modify Custody.

How Is Child Support Determined?

Child support is a statutory right of the child or children, not the custodial parent. Past and present child support can be waived; however, future child support cannot be waived. Additionally, the court enforces this obligation against the parent who is required to pay.

An experienced child support attorney can assist you in calculating your child support obligation if you will be the party making child support payments, or your spouse's child support obligation if they will be the party making child support payments to you. The most crucial point is that your child support and family law attorney can help you reach a better result or structure on child support.

Paternity

In some divorce cases or legal separations, before the issues of child custody and child support can even be decided, the parties may dispute the paternity (or parentage) of one or more minor children. Determining whether the husband is the child's father will affect the husband's and child's rights. A paternity suit will likely prolong the standard divorce process.

What Is Paternity?

Paternity is legal fatherhood, and a paternity suit is the process of establishing the legal father of a minor child. In a marriage, the husband is legally presumed to be a father of a child conceived with or born by his wife during the marriage. In case of dispute or where the child is conceived or born when the parties are not married, paternity must be established by a signed acknowledgement of paternity filed with the appropriate state agency or by establishing paternity through court action.

Who Has Custody of a Child Born Outside of Marriage?

The mother of a child born out of wedlock has sole custody of the child until a court determination of paternity.

What Legal Rights Does a Father Have Without a Paternity Determination?

Under some state laws, fathers do not have legal rights or obligations concerning a child until a court-ordered paternity determination. In those states, signing the birth certificate along with an admission of paternity will not be sufficient to exercise rights as a father.

What Are the Benefits of a Paternity Suit?

A child with a legal father can receive the benefits of that relationship. Fathers with a paternity order can assert their rights and seek child custody or the right to child visitation. Furthermore, fathers can seek decision-making authority over their children, which is the ability to participate in important decisions affecting the child's education, upbringing, extracurricular activities, etc.

Protective Orders

Unfortunately, in some divorce cases or legal separations, violence or the potential for violence may require one party to seek legal intervention to keep them, their children or other people living in their home safe from the other party. Seeking a court order to restrict the ability of one party to interact with the other necessarily complicates the divorce process. Still, such an order is often essential for one party's safety and survival.

What Are the Grounds for a Protective Order?

A protective order can usually be obtained if the person seeking the order has been a victim of domestic abuse, stalking, harassment, or rape. A protective order can also be obtained for minor children, incompetent adults, or members of the victim's household.

Where Can a Protective Order Be Filed?

A petition for a protective order may be filed in the county where the victim resides, the county where the defendant resides, or the county where the conduct leading to the petition being filed occurred.

Does the Other Side Have to Be Present at the Hearing?

If an emergency *ex parte* (meaning "without the other party") order is sought, the court holds a hearing on the same day without the respondent present. The court then issues an emergency *ex parte* order if it finds such an order to be necessary to protect the victim from the immediate danger of domestic abuse, stalking, or harassment.

Can I Seek a Protective Order Against the Other Party?

Yes, you may seek a protective order against the party that originally filed for a protective order against you, if you qualify as a victim of domestic abuse, stalking, harassment, or rape.

Can I Ask for a Protective Order at the Hearing?

You should file a petition for a protective order if you qualify before the hearing on a protective order sought against you.

Who Hears the Protective Order If I Have a Divorce or Custody Action Pending?

Generally, the judge assigned to hear the protective order transfers the protective order to the judge hearing your custody, divorce, or other family law case. Additionally, if you have a protective order case pending in one county and a family law, divorce, or custody matter pending in another county, state procedural rules typically require the court hearing the protect order action to transfer it to the existing family law court.

What Are the Consequences of a Protective Order?

Among other things, the court may transfer custody of minor children to the petitioner (the person seeking the protective order) while the protective order is effective. The judge may also require the person against whom a protective order is entered to forfeit possession of firearms, and their employment may be affected.

SECTION 4: EARLY STAGES OF DIVORCE

"The best, kindhearted attorneys and staffing. I highly recommend Cannon and Associates for any of your needs! I was referred by a good friend of mine and they definitely did everything for me, even walked me through each and every step start to finish."

Justin

First Step to Divorce–Confidential Strategy Session

Beginning the process is often the most difficult part when facing separation or divorce. An experienced family law attorney should have a well-developed process to assist you in learning about divorce, making the first key decisions, and taking your first confident step on the journey to your new life.

Your chosen divorce attorney can greatly assist or hurt you in setting the tone and temperament of your divorce. A divorce attorney's retainer and billable hour rate are not the most important factors in deciding what attorney to trust with your case. In other words, the most expensive divorce lawyer is not necessarily the best. In the divorce, it is essential to know that the family law attorney you hire understands your concerns and is dedicated to your goals, not their own goals.

You spend a substantial amount of time working with the divorce attorney you hire. You must know, like, and trust the family law firm you chose to work with on your divorce. Your future, your finances, and your peace of mind rest, in part, on your divorce attorney. So, read reviews and testimonials, study divorce lawyer websites, and hire the divorce attorneys you feel are best for you and your situation. Meeting with and researching several family law attorneys before deciding is critical. It is in your interest financially and strategically to work with one divorce attorney through your entire case, so choose wisely.

Once you have selected an attorney you believe you want to work with, an initial confidential strategy meeting assists you in answering your questions, learning the basic process and framework of divorce, and learning about your options.

During a confidential strategy meeting, you can expect the following:

INTRODUCTION: The first and most crucial step in beginning your search for a divorce attorney is meeting with the legal team and determining if you like and trust them to represent you in your divorce. The attorney should be explicit that the consultation is a confidential conversation and that the information discussed is not shared with anyone. You should be prepared to answer several questions to ensure the attorney understands your concerns and your goals in your case.

LISTEN: The attorney should listen carefully to your concerns, fears, and desired outcomes for your case and help you set aggressive yet reasonable goals for your divorce. By isolating the areas of family law that apply to your situation, the attorney can maximize your time together by giving only relevant and useful legal advice.

EDUCATE: The major issues in most divorce proceedings consist of some or all the following issues: legal custody of children, physical custody of children, division of assets, division of debts, spousal support, and child support. Although this is not an exhaustive list, most issues in divorce cases fall under one of these categories or are related issues. During the initial confidential strategy session, an experienced family attorney should assist you in understanding both these general issues and how they apply to your divorce. You will benefit most if you have an attorney who can explain the process and rules straightforwardly and avoid complex legal theory and legalese.

ADVISE: An experienced family law attorney should provide you valuable insight and advice for your specific situation and provide specific legal advice on your specific pain points and concerns. The level of detail in your consultation depends on the information you want to receive. Whether you choose to work with the attorney or not, you should leave your meeting in the best possible position to succeed in your divorce.

GAME PLAN: After your case strategy consultation, you should have a better understanding of the issues and options you face in your divorce, professional input/feedback on your objectives, and a roadmap to reaching your goals in all the issues in your divorce case. The attorney may also help you develop a game plan for your divorce, including whether to proceed without counsel, wait for a more opportune time, develop a specific negotiation strategy, attempt marital counseling, or immediately file your divorce action to protect your financial interests or child custody.

Whatever your circumstances, you should hopefully leave your initial confidential strategy session knowing your options, the foreseeable risks in your divorce, and the attorney's legal fees for representing you.

Considerations Before Discussing Divorce with Your Spouse

Before you open a topic of conversation that cannot be shut - divorce – you want to consider several key issues. You may use the confidential strategy session to work through some of the questions with an experienced attorney.

The following are important questions to consider:

- Do you know what you want in the divorce?
- Can you intelligently explain why you want a divorce?
- Have you considered how your spouse will react?
- Will your spouse hotly contest divorce?
- Do you know what custody agreement you want?
- Will your spouse agree to the child custody agreement you would want?
- Have you identified the right place and time to initiate this conversation?

Planning the time, place, and manner of telling your spouse you no longer wish to be married to them is vital. Prepare yourself for the potential issues that may arise before you open the topic of divorce with your spouse.

Practical Preparations Before Filing

In addition to thinking about how the conversation with your spouse might go and how they stand on important issues, you will want to take some concrete actions before raising the topic of divorce, which could start a race to the courthouse.

You can take action to put yourself in the best possible position to reach a fair outcome in the divorce. In this section, we summarize our key suggestions for preparing practically before raising the topic of divorce. Preparation is key in starting on a strong foot in your divorce case.

Be Mindful of the Filing Fee for Divorce

In most states, a filing fee is associated with filing any civil case, including divorce actions. Divorces with minor children typically have a higher filing fee than divorces without minor children. If you hire a divorce attorney, you should clarify whether they pay the filing fee of your divorce, or whether you are responsible for this cost. You will need to be prepared for this expense if it is not included in your attorney's fees.

Prepare Your Evidence

It can be difficult not to just walk out of your marriage and file for divorce when you decide enough is enough. However, if it is safe and you can stand it, you must collect evidence and information relevant to your divorce before leaving the marital home. You should photograph assets, make copies of every account statement you can access, write down important numbers, and document other important information for your divorce. You should set up a new Cloud, Dropbox, or Google Drive account to store this information, as well as a paper copy.

Additionally, property ownership documentation is crucial to obtaining an accurate property division. Some assets are separate property and can maintain that characteristic. Documentation concerning assets can help preserve the separate property characteristic of an asset. Many documents have a strange way of disappearing during divorce, which is why it is essential to make copies of every important document before leaving the marital home or filing for divorce. Knowledge is power and obtaining all this information greatly helps your divorce attorney present your case in the best way possible.

Know Your Spouse's Finances

You should be familiar with your spouse's financial situation prior to filing for divorce or even separation. You can begin the process by tracking your spouse's new or existing credit cards, loan applications, and the current balance and transactions of all your bank accounts. Many times, people elaborate on their income for credit or loan purposes; and provide a much more conservative number to the IRS. Loan applications and other financial information can be critical in the discovery process for your divorce case.

Get Property Valued Before You Part Ways

Property is usually on the table in a divorce. However, you may have difficulty obtaining your fair share of the property if you do not know the value of each asset. Experts are available to assess the value of every type of asset, whether it be a realtor for your marital home/other property, an appraiser for a specific asset, or a financial analyst or forensic accountant for determining the value of a business.

Know Your Debt Obligations

The name of the party on the debt is not the sole factor used to determine what is marital debt as opposed to personal or separate debt. Many factors contribute to this determination. When considering paying down debt before filing for divorce or during the divorce process, ensure that you are paying down marital debt to the extent possible, not the other party's personal debt. You want to ensure that you cannot be viewed as responsible for debts that the court may determine are the sole responsibility of your spouse.

Understand the Timing of Changes in Asset Values

It is essential to know that the date of separation may determine property division in your divorce. Family courts typically use your formal date of separation to determine property division and the value of marital. Some assets have set dates for increases or decreases in value; you may want to take note of these dates when deciding the date for your divorce filing. Although it may be tempting to file for divorce as soon as possible, there are financial interests in many circumstances in waiting to file for divorce. You should wait to trigger the formal date of separation until it is beneficial to you, if possible, such as a known date of an increase, or likely increase, in the value of a stock or an investment that will undergo an increase in value, such as a dividend or stock split.

Plan Your Financial Wellbeing Beyond Divorce

Clients often neglect to consider how their financial planning can change after a divorce. You likely have a different perspective on finances and investments than your spouse, which is part of why it is so important to identify your plan for financial success after divorce. In most marriages, one party handles all the finances. You may want to work with a financial planner, at least temporarily, if you were never responsible for planning finances during the marriage.

You should prepare for the potential of seeking employment if your spouse currently supports you. That may require updating your resume or seeking new job training. You may be awarded some spousal support or alimony to provide for your needs after divorce for a limited time and amount. However, relying entirely on this outcome is not wise – don't put all your eggs in one basket. You can continue to seek spousal support or alimony while seeing employment to support yourself beyond divorce. Improving your job skills or education can protect you from being completely reliant on alimony, which is empowering in and of itself.

You should also take steps to research and identify health insurance resources if your spouse is currently providing insurance for you. Your post-divorce options for continuing coverage may be expensive (such as COBRA coverage) or limited (such as TRICARE for military spouses). Whether or not you find new employment that provides health insurance, it is vital to be proactive in researching health insurance options, if necessary, for after divorce.

Ensure Your Safety and Your Children's Safety

Fortunately, most divorces do not involve domestic violence; however, those that do can be deadly. You should seek assistance from the court or your divorce attorney if violence may be an issue in your divorce. Victim Protective Orders (VPO) are available for victims of domestic violence and can protect you from any unwanted direct contact with your spouse during the divorce process. In most family courts, the judges combine the VPO and divorce proceedings to minimize the number of court appearances and allow one judge to review and decide all the issues in your case. If your safety or your children's safety may be at risk, you should speak to your chosen family law attorney about a Victim Protective Order.

Wise divorce attorneys advise you to do your homework and prepare prior to filing for divorce. We advise you to do as much homework as possible before raising the subject with your spouse, as certain actions, such as gathering documents, can be much more difficult once your spouse knows you are contemplating divorce. You may think these actions could tip your spouse off about your intentions, but when done carefully, this preparation can put you in the best position to protect your interests.

How to Tell Your Spouse You Want a Divorce

After you have developed a game plan, including determining that divorce is your best option, and made practical preparations, you will want to consider carefully when and how to tell your spouse that you want a divorce. This section gives you some suggestions for how to approach this potentially difficult conversation. If violence is an issue in your marriage, please approach the conversation even more carefully or consult with an attorney or victims' advocate organization for how to proceed without this conversation.

Initiating the Conversation

Is There a Right Way to Tell Your Spouse You Want a Divorce?

I'm often asked if there is a right way to tell your spouse you want a divorce. The answer to the question is "maybe," but there is definitely a *wrong* way to tell your spouse you want a divorce.

Consider Your Feelings and Their Feelings

You and your spouse have already lived part or much of your lives together. You may have children together, but you certainly have good and bad memories. Your marriage, your life together, and your history are uniquely yours and yours alone. There is no script for every divorce because every marriage, and consequently every divorce, is different.

Discussing divorce can and often does bring up sensitive issues for your spouse: shock, denial, anger, resentment, depression, jealously, and emotions you may have never seen from them. The best thing you or anyone can do in this situation is to not make a difficult situation worse.

An experienced divorce attorney would tell you to begin this conversation only when you are ready to deal with various possible responses. You know your spouse better than anyone does—factor in their personality and emotions in deciding when and where to bring up this very personal and difficult subject. You can plan for the worst, and you should.

Help with the Conversation – Marriage Counseling

One way to plan for the emotional response to divorce and related issues is to seek marriage counseling. Often a spouse is totally caught off guard concerning the depth of pain an issue has caused their spouse. If this is the case, and you are willing to work on the issue together before filing for divorce, marriage counseling is a great idea. Many resources are available for marriage counseling, whether through your place of worship, a licensed mental health professional, a counselor, or another source; consider this option to save your marriage before filing for divorce. Every day, spouses considering divorce or already in divorce proceedings decide to reconcile.

You can benefit from marriage counseling even if you believe you and your spouse are beyond reconciliation, either emotionally or because you are already physically separated. Speaking to an experienced professional can help you and your spouse identify issues or communication failures not identified before. Whether or not divorce is inevitable, learning how to better communicate with your spouse makes both your lives easier in marriage or during and after divorce.

Topics to Discuss

Staying or Leaving the Marital Home

It is very unusual, but possible, for both parties to live in the marital home after divorce. The overwhelming majority of divorce proceedings involve one party leaving the marital home during the divorce. You need to know if you are willing to leave the house before telling your spouse you want a divorce. You also need to know if your spouse wants to stay or go.

It is crucial to your mental health and finances to keep or sell your marital home for the right reasons. You may have a strong emotional tie to your marital home; however, you should consider whether it is good or bad for your continued mental health to live in the house after divorce. After divorce, you do not want to discover that you gave up assets that mean more to you just to keep a marital home that you do not really want or cannot afford.

You could be stuck with the bill of not only maintaining the marital home during your divorce proceeding but also an apartment or townhome for you or your spouse. You need to take time for additional planning if you have minor children and hope to have them stay with you some or all the time you are in your new home.

Child Custody and Parenting Time

As a parent, I know the most important question for almost every parent is this: Who will your children spend most of their time with during and after divorce? The home you make for yourself and your children during and after divorce plays a major role in the time your children spend with you. Children need a bedroom, or at least an area of your home, that is theirs. Many parents lose the opportunity to have their children live with them simply because of logistics that prevent them from making a place for their children.

Children often spend more time with the parent that remains in the marital home during the divorce, largely because of the stability it affords. Children who stay in the marital home remain close to friends, attend the same school generally, attend the same place of worship, remain in the community they know, and so on. You should advocate for keeping the marital home if you want your children to spend most of their time with you.

Regardless of whether you stay or leave the marital home, during the divorce, a parenting plan will be put in place by agreement or by order of the court. The plan dictates who has "final decision-making authority," among many other important issues. Because the issues related to child custody and parenting plans affect your life and your children's lives for many years, you may wish to consult with a family law attorney before having these discussions with your spouse.

Where to File

It is more difficult in some states than in others to seek a divorce. If you and your spouse agree to divorce, you may want to consider leaving your state and moving to a state where the process is more straightforward. For example, in Oklahoma, if you have established residency so that the court has jurisdiction, you can obtain a divorce in ten days without children and only ninety days if you have minor children. Additionally, the ninety-day waiting period can be waived under some circumstances.

Principles to Consider

Nowhere in the law do you find the way to tell your spouse you want a divorce. However, family law does contain language dealing with fairness and equity. When discussing divorce and related issues with your spouse, you can and should consider the following general principles:

- The relative circumstances of each spouse are essential in the determinations of spousal support both during the divorce process and after the divorce. Courts consider two factors: 1) the need of the spouse seeking support, and 2) the ability of the other spouse to provide support.

- Courts determine child custody based on what is "in the best interest of the child." The court in your custody case is not allowed to exercise a preference for the mother or the father. You should approach this issue with patience and understand you will likely have continued contact with your spouse, at least concerning custody of your children, until all your children are adults, if not beyond. Even if you or your spouse are awarded sole physical custody, the other parent generally has the right to continued regular visitation unless physical abuse, sexual abuse, or substance abuse is an issue.

- In many states, most divorces are settled without trial, through mediation, saving time, money, and heartache about an uncertain outcome. Remember that you may have to negotiate with your spouse before you refuse to discuss terms with them.

- Division of property is usually required to be "equitable." Accordingly, courts may look unfavorably upon attempts to deprive one spouse of their equitable share.

- Divorce is not final until it is final. Additionally, states prevent you from marrying anyone else for a specified period after your divorce is final (for example, six months in Oklahoma). You and your spouse can work through your issues at any time until the final decree is entered, and no divorce attorney should ever try to convince you not to reconcile with your spouse.

Fairness and equity are paramount in divorce proceedings, which makes sense as the issues in divorce—child custody, separation, and division of your property—are very personal. Divorce courts and judges focus on the child's best interest first, the fairness to the parties second, and everything else after these two considerations. This concept of fairness begins with how you first communicate with your spouse. Being mean-spirited or intentionally hurtful does you no good and may cost you in the process.

When facing divorce, it is very easy to be motivated by anger, sadness, or revenge. However, this focus has a very negative effect on your finances and may hurt your case. When you ask your divorce attorney to draft a demand letter or email to the opposing party in your divorce regarding every wrongdoing, you end up spending thousands of dollars in unnecessary attorney fees. Knowing how quickly a divorce case becomes expensive will hopefully help you pick your battles. If you are dedicated to fighting every issue in your divorce, you must be prepared to pay substantial retainer fees.

Alternatively, you can preserve your finances and mental health by compromising on some issues. When tempted to fight every issue in your divorce, remember the benefits to your health and your pocketbook of agreeing to compromise. Additionally, your decision to compromise on some issues may result in your spouse doing the same and simplifying your divorce.

You are not likely to reach the exact outcome you want in your divorce case. However, when contemplating divorce, it is important to identify the battles you care about the most and prepare to let other issues go. You should avoid attorney fees and fighting over issues that you do not care about deeply. Take time to think and communicate with your divorce attorney to ensure that you and your legal team are on the same page with your goals and concerns in your divorce case.

Advantages of Being the First to File for Divorce

In most divorce cases, one spouse files their Petition to begin the process. The decision to file your Petition for Divorce should never be taken lightly. However, if your mind is made up and you are going to seek a divorce, there may be advantages to being the first party to begin the process.

The following are the five most common benefits of first initiating a divorce. Each of these reasons should be considered before deciding to file for divorce; however, not all apply to every divorce.

1. Controlling Timing for Automatic Temporary Injunctive Relief

Oklahoma law imposes mandatory injunctions (ATIs) on both parties to a divorce from the moment the Petition for divorce is filed.

The primary purpose of the automatic temporary injunctions is to stop each spouse from taking actions to hurt the marital estate, divest the other of marital property, or affect the children and the other spouse without agreement between both parties or a court order. The spouse who files the Petition also determines when these ATIs go into effect.

2. Starting the Clock

The clock for resolving your case cannot start until you have filed your Petition for divorce. Most state laws require a minimum period between filing the Petition and the final decree. For example, an uncontested divorce can be settled ten days after filing in Oklahoma if no minor children are involved. When minor children are involved, at least ninety days must pass before a judge finalizes a divorce in Oklahoma.

3. Going First at Trial

In civil litigation practice, which applies to divorce, the party that filed the original Petition seeking a divorce presents their case first at trial. In some circumstances, this can give you an advantage at trial. First impressions are important in most things in life, which often applies at trial in divorce cases.

The majority of divorces are settled between the parties, either by agreement or mediation; however, it is good to know if your divorce case must go to trial, you will have the first opportunity to tell your story to the judge with the help of your divorce attorney.

4. Dismissal Based on Reconciliation

Many divorces are dismissed based on the parties reconciling or their desire to attempt reconciliation. Only the party that files the Petition for divorce can dismiss the case if you reconcile before your spouse files a counterclaim or answer.

As the first to file, you control whether the case is dismissed or proceeds, which may be a useful advantage in your attempts at reconciliation.

5. Strategy

Finally, initiative can sometimes be to your strategic advantage. Many family law attorneys believe the party that files the Petition has an initial advantage. This point, as is the case for most opinions, can be and is hotly contested by attorneys and parties to divorce. However, you certainly set the tone in your case if your family law judge reads your Petition prior to the other side's claims in your divorce.

This list of potential advantages to filing your Petition for divorce before your spouse files does not apply to every divorce or situation. You must speak to an experienced family law attorney to know the best course of action for you and your case.

What to Do After Being Served with Divorce

Unfortunately, you may not be the first to file a Petition because your spouse beats you to the courthouse. Even when things are not going well in your marriage, it is always a shock to be served with a petition for divorce. When you are served with a divorce petition, failing to act is planning to fail. If you have received a petition for divorce from your spouse, you must overcome the shock and act quickly. Below are the most important immediate actions to take to protect your legal rights and interests when you are served with divorce.

1. Read the Petition for Divorce

Although you may presume to know the content of the papers that have just been delivered to you, it won't hurt to go through the details of the divorce petition. Carefully reading the papers can provide you with a wealth of information, including the court where the action was initiated, the deadline for your response, and whether the initiating party is acting alone or with help from an attorney.

As part of the information in the papers, you will also find the legal grounds for divorce and specific requests, such as child support, spousal support, property division, child custody, and other pertinent issues. You may be able to identify your spouse's goals in the divorce and what they care the most about in the process. Developing a clear understanding of your spouse's position in the petition assists you in developing a good strategy for responding to the divorce petition.

2. Hire a Divorce Attorney

The divorce process can go in many different directions, and the process itself may bog you down without experienced divorce counsel. You will likely miss certain opportunities in your case if you lack the proper understanding of the laws and rules governing divorce. It is in your interest to hire an experienced family lawyer when you can. The cost of hiring an experienced divorce attorney is far less than the money you are likely to lose over time from paying too much alimony or child support, turning over too much property, or giving up retirement funds.

Your chosen divorce attorney will go through the Petition, and educate you on what each request means and what it translates into the long term. Additionally, an experienced divorce attorney can advise you of the best course of action and alternative options at every step of the divorce process.

It is essential for you to retain the services of an experienced divorce attorney if your spouse has retained one. Failing to retain an experienced divorce attorney's services puts you at the mercy of your spouse's legal team during the case. Family law is a court of equity; however, the game is not fair if you do not have an equal or better legal team than your spouse.

3. Respond to the Divorce Petition

In carefully reading the document, you'll find the deadline by which your response is required. For example, in Oklahoma, you have twenty days from the date you were served the divorce petition to respond by filing an answer and counter-petition. Take care to note the deadline correctly since missing it can mean forfeiture of the opportunity to seek certain relief in the divorce process or even having a default divorce entered against you. If you hire a divorce attorney, they will draft your response to each request based on your desired outcome and represent your interests if the case later becomes contested.

However, if you cannot afford to hire a family lawyer within the time required to respond, you may prepare and file your response. In your response, you must state your answer to each allegation or request of your spouse.

4. Gather Important Documents

If you have contacted a divorce attorney, they will ask you to gather necessary documents that can be used to ascertain your finances and protect you. Common documents requested include birth certificates, bank statements, credit card statements, tax returns over the last three years, and investment documents. These documents help your legal team to identify your income, debt, tax, assets, and more.

5. Protect your Assets

As part of the divorce process, asset protection is essential. Discuss with your family law attorneys how you can protect your assets and maximize what you take out of the divorce. If you own a joint account with your spouse, you can withdraw as much as 50% of the amount in the account before it is frozen as part of the divorce process. So, withdraw those funds as soon as you are served. You also need to change where your income is deposited if it currently goes directly into the joint account. In general, your divorce lawyer works closely with you to ensure your finances and assets are protected.

6. Protect Communications

Your voice and electronic communication during the divorce process are important. You should ensure that you change passwords and put in place strict measures to safeguard information exchanges between you and your divorce attorneys. It helps if you can also keep information about your divorce away from the internet. You likely have many passwords that your spouse knows or could easily guess, so it is important to set new passwords that your spouse would not know and that you have not used before. Change your passwords on every social media, email, and other accounts. You probably want to open a brand-new email account and use only that account for all potentially sensitive communication, especially when communicating with your divorce attorney.

Even when the petition for divorce comes as a surprise, if you take the steps we suggest, you will be better prepared to defend your interests in the divorce proceedings.

You should upload your texts and phots to Dropbox, Google Drive, or email them to yourself (preferably a new email account). This simply process will allow you to protect your evidence in a safe way, which does not rely on your smart phone. Cloud storage with the right safeguards is always safer than simply relying on your phone, which can be lost, stolen, or damaged.

What does the Court do once the Petition is Filed?

When you or your spouse files a petition for divorce, the court will take-action to make sure that both parties to the divorce are protected. The main tool the court uses to protect those parties is to issue court orders, which prohibit you and your spouse from doing certain things and require you to do certain other things.

Some orders are automatic, meaning the court issues them in every divorce proceeding. Knowing how these automatic orders will affect you, your spouse, and your minor children is important before you file for divorce.

Other orders are in the court's discretion, meaning one party must request the order, and the court decides whether the order is justified. It is essential to understand what options you have so that you may request any additional orders that may be necessary in your case.

Automatic Temporary Injunctions

Automatic Temporary Injunctions (ATI) prohibit both spouses from engaging in a large variety of conduct, which may or may not hurt the other party's interests. In order to take-action outside of the injunctions, the spouse would need a court order or agreement by the other party.

Automatic Temporary Injunctions go into effect against both parties as soon as the Petition is served on the respondent and remain in effect until the final divorce decree is entered or the Petition is dismissed or until the court issues a different order.

Two exceptions exist: (1) both parties can waive the need for ATI or (2) one party files an objection with the court and requests a hearing on one or more ATI. In the latter case, the challenged order(s) remain in effect until the court hearing.

ATI typically prevent both parties to the divorce from taking the following actions:

- Harassing the other party or the children of the marriage.
- Taking children out of any school, program, or day-care where the children historically have been enrolled.
- Hiding the children from the other party.
- Taking the children out of state, whether directly or with the help of others, except for vacations of a maximum length (often no more than two weeks), without the prior written consent of the other party.
- Disposing of, mortgaging, or hiding any marital property without the written consent of the other party or a court order, except:

  (A) in the usual course of operating a business;

  (B) to retain an attorney for the case; or

  (C) for the necessities of life.

- Intentionally or knowingly damaging or destroying any tangible property of either spouse.
- Taking money out of any retirement or other employee benefit plan or employee savings plan or from any individual retirement account or Keogh account.
- Withdrawing or borrowing against life insurance policies or changing any life or other insurance policy (such as health, property, vehicle, homeowners') that covers either spouse, their children, or their property.
- Opening or diverting mail addressed to the other party.
- Signing or endorsing the other spouse's name on any negotiable instrument, check, or draft attempting to cash out any negotiable

instruments payable to either party without the personal signature of the other party.

ATI also require each spouse to deliver several documents to the other spouse within a specified period after service of the Petition on the respondent (often thirty days). These documents typically include:

- Tax returns and all supporting documentation for the tax returns
- Recent pay stubs from each employer for whom the party worked.
- Statements for all bank accounts held by either party individually or jointly for the benefit of either party or held by either party for the benefit of the minor child or children of the parties.
- Documentation regarding all debts in the name of either party individually or jointly, showing the most recent balance due and payment terms.
- Documentation about health insurance coverage for the benefit of either party, the minor child or children of the parties.
- Documentation of certain childcare expenses incurred for the benefit of the minor child or children of the parties.

State laws provide instructions for how to comply with these requirements when a document is unavailable, which usually means providing a signed affidavit. The parties also must supplement their document disclosures as new information becomes available.

Because the actions and documents covered by ATI are numerous, it is a good idea to consult with an attorney before you file for divorce or quickly after you've been served with divorce papers so that you understand what you cannot do and what documents you are required to produce. The court does have the power to punish you for violations of its orders.

Victim Protective Orders

The Victim Projective Order or VPO is a tool in state court intended to protect victims of violence, stalking, rape, domestic violence, and harassment. A VPO provides a legal process to protect both women and men from abusive or harassing behavior by those with a current or former close relationship with the victim. Once a VPO is in place, it provides protections through potential civil and criminal penalties if the VPO is violated by the person whose actions it restricts.

In divorce cases where there is a history of violence or harassment in the marriage or the possibility of violence or harassment during the divorce. The following is a brief explanation of the VPO process and rules governing eligibility for a VPO.

Overview of Eligibility for a Victim Protective Order

The following individuals are generally eligible to seek a protective order:

- The victim of stalking;
- The victim of harassment;
- The victim of domestic abuse;
- The victim of rape; or

To seek a VPO against an individual, a relationship or specific acts must occur.

For a relationship to qualify for the purposes of a VPO, the parties must be connected as follows: married, former spouses, present spouse of former spouse, dating relationship, former dating relationship, child-parent, biological parents of the same child, related by marriage, or living in the same household.

A "dating relationship" typically requires an intimate association, primarily characterized by affectionate or sexual involvement and excludes casual acquaintances or ordinary business or social interactions.

Certain victims can obtain a VPO against their aggressors regardless of the relationship between the parties: rape victims, victims of forcible sodomy, victims of other sex offenses, kidnapping victims, victims of assault and battery with a deadly weapon, and immediate family members of victims of murder.

To seek a VPO, you must determine what court has jurisdiction over the petition. In most cases, you may choose among the county where you reside, the county where the person you are seeking protection from resides, or the county where the act that is the basis for your petition occurred.

To justify the need for a VPO, you must show that the defendant's conduct includes:

1) attempting or causing physical harm;
2) threatening imminent physical harm;
3) stalking; or
4) harassment

You must file a police report prior to filing a VPO, if the basis of your VPO petition is stalking. Additionally, you will need to attach the police report to your petition for protective order based on stalking.

A Closer Look at Eligibility

It is important to understand what constitutes "stalking," "harassment," or "domestic abuse" under the law. You will want to speak with an attorney or victim services in your county to make sure you understand these terms and determine whether your situation qualifies you to seek a VPO.

The following is a summary of how these terms are commonly defined, but again small state law variations may be the difference between being eligible and being ineligible.

Stalking

Stalking typically involves unconsented and menacing contact that occurred multiple times within a certain period.

The law typically requires "willful, malicious, and repeated" contact "that would cause a reasonable person to feel frightened, intimidated, threatened, harassed, or molested." (See, for example, Oklahoma Statutes Title 22 Section 60.1.)

Additionally, this conduct must cause the victim to feel frightened, intimidated, etc. There is an objective assessment – would a "normal" person be scared – and a subjective assessment – is the victim genuinely scared.

To constitute stalking, the contact must include at least two separate instances that show a sustained purpose without the victim's consent or ignoring the victim's explicit desire not to be contacted. The types of contact include both in-person and electronic and indirect contact. A short and incomplete list is below:

- following or appearing within sight of the victim;

- approaching or confronting the victim in a public place or on private property;

- appearing at the workplace or residence of the victim;

- entering onto or remaining on property owned, leased, or occupied by the victim;

- contacting the victim by telephone;

- sending mail or electronic communications to the victim; or

- placing an object on, or delivering an object to, property owned, leased, or occupied by the victim.

Harassment

Harassment is somewhat similar to stalking, but there are substantial differences. Harassment requires a pattern of conduct that irritates or distresses a person and is without a legitimate purpose.

The law typically requires "a knowing and willful course or pattern of conduct ... that seriously alarms or annoys the person and serves no legitimate purpose (see, for example, Oklahoma Statutes Title 22 Section 60.1). The perpetrator of this conduct must have a prior relationship with the victim, such as family, household member or current or past romantic relationship.

As with stalking, harassment has an objective (irritating, alarming to a reasonable person?) assessment and a subjective (irritating, alarming to the actual victim) assessment.

Domestic Abuse

For a VPO, domestic abuse typically means physical harm or imminent threat of physical harm committed by an intimate partner, family member, or household member against another. To distinguish domestic abuse from child abuse, statutes may include a minimum age for the eligible victim.

It is important to note that family and household members are defined more broadly than the nuclear family to include, for example, grandparents or cousins. The definition also includes blood and legal relationships, such as marriage (e.g., stepparents or stepchildren), adoption, or foster care.

How Can I Get a Victim Protective Order?

There are generally two procedures for obtaining an initial temporary VPO: emergency ex-parte orders and emergency *temporary* ex-parte orders. The term ex parte means that an order is granted without the presence of the person against whom the order is sought (the defendant). The main difference between these two types of orders is who grants the VPO, a court or law enforcement.

For an emergency ex parte VPO the victim petitions a court during normal business hours. Typically, the paperwork is available at the court clerk's office. The document is simply called a "Petition for Protective Order."

Once the paperwork is completed, the court holds an ex-parte hearing, meaning a hearing without the defendant present, and decides if sufficient grounds have been presented to enter an ex-parte order against the defendant. The court only issues an emergency ex-parte order if it finds an imminent and present danger of domestic abuse, stalking, harassment, or if a qualifying sexual assault has occurred. Once served upon the defendant, the emergency order has full force and effect until the full VPO hearing at which the Defendant appears.

If the Defendant has been served with the emergency protective order and fails to appear at the protective order hearing, the emergency order stays in full force and effect. However, a final protective order will sometimes be denied, if service cannot be obtained against the Defendant to the protective order. Conversely, the VPO will be dismissed, if the Petitioner does not appear at the hearing.

Victims may seek an emergency *temporary* ex-parte order when the courthouse is closed if they are the victim of domestic violence, stalking, harassment, rape, forcible sodomy, a sex offense, kidnapping, assault and battery with a deadly weapon, or a family member of a murder victim.

To initiate this process, a victim must contact law enforcement or police and present information to support the basis for the emergency ex-parte *temporary* victim protective order. Law enforcement officers have access to county judges to seek permission to grant these types of protective orders when courthouses are closed; however, the emergency *temporary* order is valid only until a hearing before a judge, which must occur within fourteen days of issuance of the emergency temporary order.

Victim Protective Order Hearing

Victim Protective Order hearings must be scheduled within fourteen days of filing the Petition for Protective Order; however, the court has the authority to schedule a full VPO hearing within seventy-two hours of the issuance of an emergency ex-parte order. Fortunately, or unfortunately, depending on which side of the protective order you are on, an emergency VPO can suspend visitation rights with your children, even children in your home for whom you are a custodial parent, if the court enters an order that applies to minor children.

Petitions for a VPO renew every fourteen days, with a new hearing date scheduled until the VPO Defendant is served, meaning the emergency order remains valid until the hearing occurs. The order will not be dismissed or expire simply because the defendant avoids service or fails to appear at the hearing. However, the Petitioner to a VPO can ask the court to dismiss the Petition. The court must enter an order dismissing the VPO for its effect to end. Additionally, a final protective order is granted or denied within six months of service on the Defendant, unless the parties agree for the temporary VPO to remain in effect.

How to Prepare for Your Victim Protective Order Hearing

The first step towards success in seeking a protective order or defending yourself against a victim protective order is to retain competent counsel.

You will be better prepared to present your case or your defense if you have an experienced VPO attorney. If obtaining a VPO is an issue as you prepare for your divorce filing, you will want to ensure that your divorce attorney has this experience.

The next step to prepare for your VPO hearing is to discuss in detail with your attorney how to best present evidence to support your victim protective order or what you can present to defend against the victim protective order. You may find you can strengthen your VPO case by presenting witnesses, exhibits, or evidence to support your case. You will be held to the rules of evidence whether you retain counsel or not, and it will be easier to ensure the evidence you want to be presented to the court is admitted if you have experienced counsel assisting you in presenting your case.

There are many elements in a compelling story to support or defend against a victim protective order; however, thinking through your strategy is an integral part of identifying what evidence you want to present, how you present it, and what you need to do for it to be deemed admissible.

What Happens at the VPO Hearing?

VPO hearings are similar to civil trials because both sides are permitted to present evidence to support their position. The Petitioner of the VPO has the burden of proof, therefore, they go first. The Petitioner may present witnesses and evidence to support the request for a protective order. After the Petitioner presents their case, the Defendant may defend against the imposition of a protective order by presenting their evidence. Both parties are allowed to attack or cross-examine the witnesses presented by the other party. This is one of many aspects of a protective order that warrants retaining experienced VPO counsel. The burden of proof in the protective order is a preponderance of the evidence. The petitioner must present enough evidence to convince the judge a protective order is necessary.

The court has wide latitude to impose restrictions that the court believes decrease the risk of domestic abuse, harassment, stalking, or sexual assault by the Defendant against the Petitioner and the Petitioner's immediate family/household members. Courts tend to err on the conservative side for protective orders and place more restrictions rather than less.

Unfortunately, in our divorce and child custody practice, we have seen that protective orders are an often-abused tool to seek an upper hand in child custody proceedings. The court may assess costs and fees against the Petitioner if the court finds the protective order was frivolously filed. In case of abusive filings, the petitioner may face fines or jail time. If you sincerely need a VPO, consult an attorney to help build your case. Do not test the court's patience with frivolous filings if you are not.

Testifying at Your VPO Hearing

You will never be required to testify at your Victim Protective Order hearing; however, it is advantageous to tell your story if it does not incriminate you in a pending or potential criminal case. A court reporter records your testimony in most VPO hearings, and that information can be used against you in a criminal case. Whether you testify or not, it is important to present as much compelling and relevant evidence as possible to support or defend against a petition for a protective order.

Final Victim Protective Order Entered—What Now?

First and foremost, the defendant to the VPO is required to abide by the terms of the Order, which at a minimum includes no contact with the Petitioner and not appearing at the Petitioner's home or place of business without a civil stand by or law enforcement presence. Final protective orders can be put in place for a maximum period (five years in Oklahoma), and violating a protective order is a crime. Additionally, it is important to know that the Petitioner cannot violate the protective order, such as by contacting the defendant. Only the defendant can violate a protective order. Therefore, a defendant cannot rely on the Petitioner initiating contact as a defense against violating a protective order.

Impacts of a VPO Places Against a Defendant

The principal impact of a VPO is an order to stop contact between the Defendant and the Petitioner. However, it can have many additional impacts, including the following:

- Prohibit the Defendant from attempting or having any contact with the Petitioner by any means, including telephone, mail, email, social media, or any other means, including using a third party to contact the Petitioner;

- Prohibit the defendant from placing the Petitioner in any form of reasonable fear of bodily harm;

- Prohibit the Defendant from terminating telephone or other services used by the Petitioner without a separate court order;

- Require immediate surrender of all firearms or other dangerous weapons; and/or

- Require obtaining domestic abuse counseling or other treatment options.

This is not an exhaustive list. Meeting with an experienced victim protective order attorney is the best way to ensure you know what you are facing as a Defendant in a VPO or what you may seek as relief if you are the Petitioner seeking a VPO.

What You Can Do If Someone Files a VPO against You

Facing a VPO is a scary and understandably upsetting proposition when you have not acted in any way that justifies such an order. The amount of evidence necessary to support the entry of an emergency ex-parte VPO is low.

You must, however, obey the terms of the VPO first and seek to fight it second.

The VPO process serves a vital public service when used appropriately; however, as the defendant in a VPO, it can be scary to know how easily your reputation and freedoms can be diminished by entry of an emergency ex-parte VPO.

VPO cases can be very public with the access to court records provided by electronic records services. Anyone at any time can search a court docket, identify any person with a pending VPO and obtain a copy of the Petition supporting the Petition for VPO. VPOs are a serious matter, and it is important that you seek experienced VPO counsel to assist you in the process of contesting the entry of a final VPO.

How can a VPO be Rescinded?

Keep in mind that once granted, the VPO remains in effect until a court orders it to be rescinded. There are three possible ways the VPO will be rescinded:

- The petitioner does not put forth enough evidence to have the court believe that a protective order should be in effect (or the defendant successfully refutes the petitioner's case).
- The parties attend the hearing, and the petitioner states that they want the VPO petition dismissed. The judge then terminates the VPO

- The petitioner does not appear at the VPO hearing. The judge then terminates the VPO.

Options two and three rely on a voluntary act by the petitioner. Do not take any action preventing another party from appearing in court. Don't threaten or harass a witness with the intent to prevent them from testifying. Doing any of these things hurts your case and potentially subjects you to criminal liability.

In cases where VPO are sought, the divorce process is much more complex, and often, the discussions are more contentious. It is important to seek advice of counsel. Understanding the options for obtaining or contesting VPO is crucial to ensure your and your children's safety as well as to protect your rights against abusive VPO petitions.

During the Divorce Process

As your divorce shifts from the early planning stages to the stages where you are interacting with your spouse, their attorney and especially the court, you can increase your chances of a favorable outcome if you keep a few things in mind.

Save Money to Take Care of Yourself During Divorce

It is wise to be conservative in your spending during the divorce process. Divorce can be expensive, especially if you and your spouse fight over issues in your divorce. Your personal needs and the needs of your children are important, so set aside resources for them during the divorce as well, such as gym membership, therapy, counseling for you and your children, or other treatment or self-care, such as massages, pedicures, or weekend getaways with your children or friends.

Beware of Starting or Flaunting a New Relationship During Divorce

The law does not prohibit dating while going through divorce; in fact, it is quite common. However, that does not mean it is necessarily a good idea. When the new love interest is the cause of seeking divorce, that relationship makes your divorce more contentious and may make reaching a settlement more difficult. Alternatively, if you and your spouse both decide to begin dating and you do not have minor children, the incentive of new love and freedom may assist in moving the divorce process along more quickly.

You should absolutely not introduce your children to your romantic interests during divorce. Your children are going through more than enough with their parents divorcing, and you introducing a new interest only makes things more difficult and stressful for your children. You should discuss this issue with your divorce attorney.

Dress Professionally for Court

Appearing in professional attire for court can only help your divorce case. The opposing party may take you more seriously, and the divorce court judge will certainly take you more seriously. Additionally, dressing for success at your divorce court hearings increases your confidence. It is important to dress in conservative clothing and not appear too flashy. Try to keep your accessories simple, and do not overdo it.

By working with a knowledgeable divorce lawyer, you obtain accurate legal advice and assistance during your divorce process. Retaining an experienced divorce attorney helps protect your property and interests while going through a stressful time.

SECTION 5: CHILDREN IN DIVORCE

"John & his team are the most professional firm in the state. From the consultation to the court room; they are true, fierce advocates. Every facet of this legal team; from receptionist to counsel, does their job exceptionally well and will treat you with respect. They traveled to southwest Oklahoma and obtained an outcome for me that I didn't dare dream. I can't find the words to express my gratitude for their service, so 5 STARS it is!!!"

Sheryl

Child Custody Overview

Often in a divorce or a legal separation, parents battle over custody of their children and the terms of their upbringing after the divorce is final. In many states, however, absent a custody order from a court, both parents are equally entitled to physical custody of any child born during the marriage or any child born to the parents prior to marriage where there is a mutual agreement the husband is the child's father. The following are some of the most common questions asked by clients facing child custody, and support issues in their divorce case:

What Does Child Custody Mean?

Child custody includes both physical custody and legal custody. Physical custody determines where and with whom each child will live after divorce. Legal custody, on the other hand, refers to a parent's right to make long-term decisions about raising the child. For example, a parent with legal custody makes decisions regarding a child's education and medical care.

A court can award sole custody or joint custody. Sole custody exists when only one parent has the right to decide where a child will live, physical custody, and decisions about raising the child, legal custody. Joint custody exists when the child lives with both parents, on an equal basis and both parents have a say on how to raise the child.

How Do You Get a Custody Order from the Court?

To get a custody order from the court, either parent must file a Petition for divorce or legal separation. Once the Petition has been filed, the court must decide whether it has authority, or "jurisdiction," to determine custody of the child. A court typically has jurisdiction over a child who has resided in the state for a specified period before filing the petition (for example, in Oklahoma, at least the past six months). When a child has not lived in the state long enough, courts might decide another state is more appropriate to determine custody.

How Does a Court Decide Which Parent to Award Custody?

Courts and experienced family law and child custody attorneys tell you that "the best interest of the child" determines child custody. The question examined by the court is what is in "the best interests of the physical, mental and moral welfare of the child." Court and judges consider the following factors in custody matters:

- The wishes of each parent and the wishes of the child (depending on the child's age);
- The quality of the relationship between the child and each parent;
- The child's relationship with grandparents, siblings, and other significant people in the child's life;
- The child's relationship to their school, religious institutions, and community;
- The mental and physical health of all parties;
- Any past, present, or possible future spousal or child abuse by either parent;
- Any past or present drug or substance abuse by either parent;
- Any past or present criminal actions by either parent (other than minor infractions or offenses that were committed a long time ago);
- Each parent's involvement in the past in getting the child to medical appointments;
- Each parent's involvement in the child's schooling;
- Each parent's ability to provide a safe home environment;
- The willingness of each parent to help foster a relationship and visitation with the other parent;
- Each parent's ability to provide a stable home life;
- Each parent's ability to provide for the child's material needs; and
- Each parent's ability to spend time with the child.

The parent not awarded physical or sole custody is often awarded certain visitation privileges. There are different types of visitations, which the court can order based on what is "in the best interest of the child."

Can You Change a Final Custody Order?

You can seek to change the final custody orders in your case by filing a "Motion to Modify Custody Order." Generally, your motion should be filed in the same court and in the same case that issued the original order. When you file such a motion, you must provide a reason that a change in the custody order is necessary. The standard to change custody orders differs depending on whether the order is a "sole custody order" or a "joint custody order." Before filing a Motion to Modify Custody Order, you should speak to an experienced child custody attorney.

A parent must demonstrate "*a permanent, material and substantial change in circumstances that affect the best interests of the child*" for a custody order to be modified in a sole custody case. The non-custodial parent has the burden of proof and must prove to the court the change in circumstances warranting a change in custody. These changes must be *significant* and *affect* the child's life. An unfortunate and common example is the presence of an abusive situation as grounds to change an order, as is neglect, or failure to care for the child, by the primary custodial parent.

A parent must show a change is "in the best interest of the minor child" to change a Joint Custody Order. A parent can seek an award of sole custody, and thereby terminate joint custody, when the parents cannot cooperate in the child's best interest. As with a change to sole custody, the parent seeking the change has the burden of proof and must prove to the court that the parties cannot cooperate and agree on what is in the child's best interest.

How Is Child Support Determined?

Child support is a child's statutory right, not the custodial parent. Past and present child support can be waived; however, future child support cannot be waived. It is a right of your child or children that the court enforces.

Generally, without court approval, parties may not agree to terminate child support.

An experienced child support attorney can assist you in calculating your child support obligation, if you will be the party making child support payments, or in calculating your spouse's child support obligation, if they will be the party making child support payments to you. Your family law attorney can help you reach a better result or structure on child support.

The rest of this section provides more details about each aspect of divorce that touches on child custody and child support and suggestions for helping your children prepare for and thrive (or at least not wither) during and after your divorce.

Leaving a Marriage When You Have Children

Being in a marriage that is not working is difficult but even more complicated when you have children. Leaving a marriage with children is not easy, as the impact extends far beyond you and your spouse. Divorce has a serious impact on children. I know personally, as I am a child of divorce. You may have pressure from family and friends to "make it work" for the children. You are likely asking yourself whether you should make your marriage work and whether your children will be happier if they can be in one or two homes with more peace.

Leaving a marriage with children should never be an impulsive decision. Additionally, the manner and timing of leaving the marriage should be after much consideration and in a way to minimize the negative impact on your children if it is safe to wait.

There is no question the divorce process may be difficult for your children; however, your children may be hurt more in the long run by living in the home of a loveless marriage. From my experience assisting many spouses facing divorce, I can tell you that children can be very happy after an unhappy divorce is finalized.

Children of all ages are smarter and more observant than we often give them credit. In marriages with a high risk of divorce, the children often recognize the imminent divorce sooner than the parents do. The National Academy of Sciences of the United States of America has completed research indicating that children often know their parents will seek divorce before it happens.

The mere act of divorce is rarely traumatic for children. Many children have been through their parents' divorce and have done just fine. What *is* traumatic for children of divorce is their personal involvement or experience in the divorce process and how well you and your spouse handle the situation.

Telling Your Children About Divorce

The following are suggestions for how to talk to your children about divorce. You will need to consider the age of each child and your relationship with them when thinking about how these suggestions apply to your situation.

Be Honest with Your Children

As mentioned previously, depending on their age, your children are likely aware that your marriage is not in good shape. Therefore, it is important to give them a clear picture of what is happening without over-informing them. You will want to determine how much detail you share based on the age of your child; so, a six-year-old may only need to know that mommy or daddy will be living in different houses; your teenager is likely mature enough to know that you and your spouse are seeking a divorce and will no longer be living together as husband and wife.

Tell Your Children About the Divorce with Your Spouse

Whether it feels this way to you or not, your children are not to blame for the divorce, even if they have impacted your marriage. They deserve to transition as smoothly as possible through this process. Therefore, presenting one concerted message to them with your spouse is important. It may be difficult to agree on what you tell your children about divorce; however, you should take the time to discuss or even argue about it before your children find out.

When Do my Children Need to Know About my Divorce?

Your children need to know about your divorce when you decide to move forward, and both parties have initially processed that a divorce action is imminent. You should not wait months after the decision to file has been made. Kids are smart; they notice that mommy or daddy are not coming home at night or not sleeping in the master bedroom.

Again, the amount of information you provide your children should be determined by their maturity and should be in a setting that reduces their likelihood of stress. For example, you may choose to tell them on the first day of a long weekend or a break from school, so they have time to process the information before returning to class. It is, however, important not to allow your children to be isolated from their friends or support network during this time. Consider what is best for your child and their maturity before determining when and where you tell your kids that you are getting divorced.

What Should I Tell My Children About Divorce?

Tell your children you are getting divorced and put it in terms that they understand without sharing the reasoning or too much detail. Ensure them at every step of the process that they are completely innocent in the situation and that you love them now as much as ever. Tell your children that just because you are getting divorced, nothing changes about how you feel about them as your children. Inform them of the new living arrangement between mom and dad and that they will always have a loving home with both parents.

If there is abuse, domestic violence, or some other factor that makes these suggestions false, then provide only as much information as necessary. Protect your children in divorce and protect their hearts.

Again, ensure at every phase of the process, beginning with the first time your children learn you are getting divorced, that they understand they are not to blame, that they have nothing to do with your decision to divorce, and that you love them. Though you may be inclined to discuss the details of your pending divorce with your children, it can only negatively impact your children and it is highly discouraged by family law courts.

Considerations on Seeking Divorce with Children

The following are tips and considerations on minimizing the negative impact of divorce on your children or your parent-child relationship.

Resolve Divorce without Fighting

During your divorce, your focus needs to be on the best interests of your children. You should immediately consult with an experienced divorce attorney if you fear your spouse will hide or kidnap your children. Please know, however, that this is a rare event and the courts and law enforcement have tools to protect you and your children if necessary. Rather than letting fears of this unlikely event guide your choices, focus on your children and their best interests.

After representing hundreds of clients facing divorce, I can assure you it is better for you and your children if custody, and your divorce in general, can be resolved without a fight. Whenever possible, it is also better to resolve these issues with the assistance of competent family law counsel. The less contention in your divorce, the less impact the process has on your children and the smoother the process is for everyone involved.

The more you and your spouse can resolve out of court, the better. Family law courts are jammed to the breaking point across the country, and you are rarely provided more than thirty minutes of court time to evaluate any issue in your divorce with children before trial. Additionally, on average, trials in divorce cases with children take over a year to be heard. All this to say, the more that can be settled in your divorce by agreement or through the assistance of experienced divorce counsel, the better.

Negotiating Your Divorce with Children

A little give and take can go a long way towards peacefully resolving your divorce with children. You should receive fair compensation and a substantial amount of time with your children in the divorce; however, remember that family courts are courts of equity. Divorce court judges across the country are tasked with reaching an outcome in the best interest of the children in the divorce, which may mean something completely different to the divorce judge than it does to you or your spouse.

Working with an experienced divorce attorney will increase your chance at best possible outcome in your divorce with children. You do not have to accept a settlement offer, or ever settle for that matter; however, it is an option that allows you to reach a more certain outcome instead of leaving your future in the hands of the judge.

Prepare Children for Divorce

In many cases, children do not understand how your divorce will impact their lives. Therefore, you and your spouse are responsible for helping them through the process. Let them know that you will be there for them no matter what and that they are not losing a parent, rather, their relationship with both parents will be different. It is important to host birthday parties and other important events together during the transition if possible and safe to do so.

Some children benefit from individual counseling during or after your divorce. You may consider providing this option if available in your area. Additionally, give your children a safe space and time to ask questions about the divorce and what their future will look like after divorce. You should focus your answers to your children's questions about divorce on what is best for them, not what puts you in the best light.

How to Get Divorced and Maintain a Relationship with Your Children

A divorce can change the direction of a parent's life. Divorce, however, does not have to be the end of your relationship with your children. You should follow the tips below to get through a divorce successfully and maintain a strong and healthy relationship with your children.

Avoid Discussing Adult Issues with or in Front of Children

It is essential to realize that your children were not the cause of the issues between you and your spouse. They are also young and may be unable to understand why their parents will not be living together anymore. Moving out may be stressful; however, it is essential to insulate your children from adult conversations about how hard this transition is on you. Whining or complaining to your kids can affect them in many ways and may negatively impact the outcome of your case if the family law judge finds out you are speaking to your children about your divorce.

If you need to have an argument or a sensitive discussion with your ex, or soon-to-be ex, you must do so outside the presence of your children. Fighting in front of the kids inspires unhealthy reactions and sets a bad example. Additionally, witnessing fights between divorcing parents can negatively impact your children for years and years to come.

Do Not Put Your Children in the Middle of Divorce

Getting your kids for a few days a week may not be enough for you. Naturally, you may want to turn your children against your ex so they can spend more time with you. This isn't right and should not be done. You should avoid making negative comments about your former spouse to your children at all costs. *Children will remember these words for the rest of their life, trust me I know from experience.*

Being pleasant when you are around your soon-to-be ex-spouse and your children is important. Remain calm and try to be pleasant when you meet for custody exchanges. Obviously, you should follow the advice of your divorce attorney and meet at a safe space, such as a police station, if safety or outbursts are a concern.

Respect your soon-to-be ex-spouse's access to your children and your children's access to them as well. Encourage your children to speak to your spouse during the divorce process, even during your visitation or time with your children, if it does not negatively impact your time with the kids. Your children are learning a new way of life. Make it as easy as possible for them by keeping lines of communication open for them either around the clock or on a routine schedule.

Don't Use Your Children for Information about Your Ex's Life

Divorced parents often use their children as private investigators. Using your children for custodial or non-custodial parent updates is a bad idea. Asking them to give an update about who your ex is with or what they noticed while there is bad parenting. You could ask about your ex's personal welfare to show them that you care, but you should never use your children as investigative tools to get personal information about your former spouse. Kids are more likely to misread and misinterpret situations that appear obvious to adults. Also, smart kids may use this dynamic as leverage to get their way by playing both parties.

Remain in Your Kids' Lives

Showing your kids that a divorce isn't enough to wipe your love for them goes a long way. Make sure to maintain a close and healthy relationship with the kids by showing up when and where they need you. Study each child, identify their interests, and build a connection around those interests. Doing this helps you to connect with them for years to come. Tell your kids and your ex far in advance if you will be unable to exercise regular visitation with your children. Life happens, and it can be beneficial to work with your ex to trade off visitation if you are unavailable for a regularly scheduled visit.

Children hate disappointments, so be sure to keep your word. Show up to their extracurricular activities as promised and make time for them when they are in your custody. Kids love spending time with loving parents, no matter how much or how little time. They are also more observant than we often give them credit and will recognize, if you are not around or active in their life.

Create New Bonds through Divorce

You can use divorce as an opportunity to create new relationships with your children by devoting space and time to them and their well-being.

The transition to seeing a parent in a new home is difficult for children of all ages. However, you can soften the blow or reduce the difficulty of the transition by making a space for your children in your new home. You should be familiar with the interests of each of your children and put some of their favorite things in your new living space or new home to help ease your child's transition.

As a result of you or your spouse moving out during the divorce, you will likely have some, or most, of your personal effects in your new living space. So, consider bringing some from the marital home or purchasing new toys or things your children will like. Of course, it is important for parents going through divorce to follow this advice within reason. You should not spend thousands of dollars on your children in your new home unless you reach an agreement with your spouse or it is financially responsible to do so.

Kids love attention and care. They want to feel safe enough to share certain parts of their day and life with you. Offering open hearts and listening ears can help you to connect better. Plan fun events for when they are around.

Invite their friends to events when necessary and spend time with them. Devoting energy and, most importantly, time to your relationship with your children benefits you and your kids for the rest of your lives. Additionally, if your children are young and you want to modify your visitation schedule, devoting time to build your relationship may be the start of your claim to change your visitation schedule.

Forgive and Move on After Divorce

Your decision to seek divorce with children is your issue and not your children's fault. Your children will know if you hold a grudge or cannot get over the divorce. They are not your counselor. Your children are not responsible for your mental health; it is the other way around. You need to get the assistance of a counselor or mental health professional if you are having difficulty letting go or forgiving your spouse. You do not need to confess your continued love or anger towards your ex to your children. That is a weight that is not theirs to bear.

In some instances, and with the assistance of marital counseling and other resources, it may be the best decision to stay in your marriage. You should consider trying to repair a broken marriage if you and your spouse are willing to try, and it is safe to do so. However, it is never the best option to simply live through a painful or loveless marriage for the sake of your children. When you know your marriage is over, you should move on to the divorce process, but do so in a way that minimizes the negative impacts of the divorce on your children.

You can build a relationship with your children during and after divorce that follows you both into their adulthood. Take the opportunity and never quit working on your relationship with your children. It serves you the rest of your life.

A Guide for Fathers Navigating Divorce

Fathers are often on the receiving end of unfavorable societal and court-ordered judgments. Many fathers already see the decks stacked against them in observing the many divorce cases around them. Not only are fathers often made out to be bad parents by their soon-to-be ex-spouses, but they also have to fight to maintain a continued relationship with their children after divorce.

Despite these skewed views and outcomes, fathers and mothers have distinct and important roles in a child's development. Children who grew up without one of their parents, whether a father or mother, are more likely to show emotional, physical, or mental vulnerability.

Fathers have the same rights as mothers in divorce proceedings. Unfortunately, in many cases, fathers get cheated out of being a part of their children's growth and development. The logistics supporting families and the pervasive view that mothers are the primary caretaker, puts fathers at a disadvantage in many divorces.

As a father going through a divorce, there may be no easy way to go through the painful process of a contested divorce. You should be aware of father's rights in divorce cases and how they may protect you. Additionally, you can take steps to maintain a loving relationship with your children and obtain the best custody or visitation arrangements in your divorce.

Know Your Rights

No parent enjoys preferential treatment during a child custody case. This means that fathers are legally allowed to petition for custody. This can be done as part of the divorce proceeding or as a stand-alone petition. In the absence of a court order that stipulates custody arrangements, both parents have equal rights to the custody of their children. If both parents cannot agree on a custody-related issue, the court determines what is in the child's best interest.

Fathers do not, however, have an automatic right to custody or visitation rights. If the child was born outside of marriage, the father is expected to accept paternity and then file a petition requesting paternity tests. The paternity test results determine the father's legal standing to file a custody and visitation case.

Courts can consider a child's preference when deciding on custody cases. It is, therefore, in your interest to maintain a good relationship with your children. However, the child's age can play an important role in whether their preferences are considered. The best interest of the child remains the primary factor the court considers.

A father can petition a court to change the terms of custody if a permanent, substantial and material change in circumstance occurs that appears to impact the child's best interest. This possibility can apply if the mother is relocating out of town, remarrying, has been arrested and convicted for criminal involvement, or has exposed your children to inappropriate circumstances, i.e. drug abuse or abuse at the hands of their significant other.

If a father has obtained a court order granting him custody, the mother cannot refuse to return the child or take the child hostage after visitation. Refusing the child's return to the father can be treated as kidnapping.

Don't Move Out

Many men feel the right thing to do is give their spouse space and time while their divorce is being processed. While this belief may come from a good place, it robs you of valuable time with your children. Additionally, moving out of the marital home before a court order increases the likelihood of the court granting your spouse temporary possession of the marital home.

Additionally, your children may see you as the father that moved out or left them with mom, an unfair interpretation of your intent. To avoid any inaccurate conclusions about your behavior, find a way to live as peacefully as possible under the same roof and with your children until the court issues a temporary court order addressing temporary custody and temporary possession of the marital home. If you cannot bear the heat at home, consult with your divorce attorney before moving out of the marital home.

Keep Detailed Records

A divorce is a life-changing event that affects the dynamics of your existing relationships. If you haven't been doing so, now is the time to begin keeping a detailed record of everything about your relationship with your children. Record how often you see your children, what you buy them, and your interactions related to the children or their welfare with your partner and others (such as teachers, doctors, coaches, and other parents).

Write down everything you can find out about your children. You may or may not have been the primary parent responsible for your children's school and extracurricular activities. However, your ability or inability to relate this information to the family law judge impacts your case. The following is a starting point for the information you should be able to collect in a journal:

- School or schools your children attend;
- The name of every teacher, doctor, and babysitter;
- Location and date of medical appointments, tutoring, and lessons;
- Knowledge of all allergies, medical conditions, mental health concerns, health concerns, and when they each began;

- Childcare providers: hours, instructors/teachers at childcare facility;
- Interests: hobbies, favorite things, activities, favorite foods;
- Dislikes: things your children won't eat; and
- Anything else you can think of about your children.

All these may come in handy later during your custody or divorce case. Protecting your interests and rights, especially your relationship with your children, should be the most important goal.

Don't Expose your Divorce Dirty Laundry

You must take the high road when dealing with a divorce. While it is understandable that you are hurting, try your best to avoid discussing the details of your divorce with others, especially on social media. Focus on working out the issue with your attorney and seek advice on every step you're to take.

Social media is a great outlet for friends and the community to discuss good and bad news; however, it is never an appropriate forum to discuss your divorce. Social media records are generally never deleted, and your spouse's divorce attorney may be able to obtain and present your hateful or inappropriate social media posts to the judge.

The same goes for text messages; I cannot tell you how many custody cases have been impacted by poorly chosen statements in text messages. Leading up to and especially during divorce, you should proceed in all forms of communication as if your words will be displayed to the judge deciding custody of your children because it happens every day.

Be on Your Best Behavior

Being reckless with your life and behavior is the worst thing to do when you feel the world is against you. The court knows that divorce is difficult and that it certainly negatively impacts your judgment. However, whenever the conduct has the potential to impact the children negatively, it can hurt your custody claim. You must maintain your cool and calm during your divorce. Always remember your decisions and actions may aggravate the stress of divorce for your children.

You may need to cease public drinking, new relationships, and other questionable behavior. I repeat: do not say it, write it, social media it, or tweet it unless you are okay with it being read by the family law judge that decides the custody of your children.

Make Time to See Your Children Often

Building a strong and healthy bond with your children can improve your relationship after the divorce is finalized. If you have moved out of the house after careful consideration or court order, make sure to see your children as often as possible, establish a new relationship with them, and fulfill any promises you make.

State laws often seek to preserve parental and children's relationships. For example, in Oklahoma, the child custody policy states:

> *Minor children will continue to have a relationship with parents who have shown the ability to act in the interest of their children. Parents are encouraged to take up joint responsibility in the care and welfare of their children after separation or divorce.*

Fathers are encouraged to honor their custody and visitation arrangement to maintain or improve their relationship with their children. Fathers should make a point to make the relationship with their children a priority.

Every year family courts and family law judges are taking a more neutral stance on preference for mothers and fathers in custody cases. What this means for you as a father is your actions and your relationship with your children play a major role in the amount of time and decision-making authority you can have in your children's lives after divorce. Applying the knowledge and suggestions above, and having a good family lawyer by your side, gives you an increased chance of receiving substantial time with your children in your divorce or custody case.

Legal Custody versus Physical Custody

One of the most common questions family law firms receive is: What is the difference between legal custody and physical custody? There are two general types of custody: legal custody and physical custody. Each of these two general types can be further broken down into joint or sole custody. Several additional custody arrangements may also be available

In this section we explain the various types of legal and physical custody.

Legal Custody

Legal custody is a determination by agreement or the court for which parent or guardian is in charge of making major life decisions for the child. Legal custody concerns major decision-making authority in your child's life, such as education, the school your child or children attend, religious upbringing, extracurricular activities, and discipline.

Legal custody does not mean the day-to-day decisions a parent makes while a child is in his or her physical custody. Who will determine the religious upbringing of the child? Who will determine what school the child attends? Who will determine what extracurricular activities that child will participate in, such as sports, music, or band? Who will decide on issues related to discipline? Many times parties will agree upon a final decision maker that will make the call on serious questions for the child. The court will enforce a primary decision maker if an agreement cannot be reached.

Types of Legal Custody

Joint Legal Custody

Joint legal custody is very common in Oklahoma. It is an arrangement where both parents are included in important decisions on the child's behalf, including healthcare decisions, education, etc. Even in joint legal custody arrangements, one parent is typically identified as the final decision maker that decides the tie if the parties are unable to settle an issue.

The parent with final decision-making authority is the parent that makes the ultimate decision in the event of a dispute. Say the parties agree that their child will play soccer but cannot decide on a recreational team or competitive travel team. The primary custodial parent decides the issue even over the objection of the other custodial parent once a discussion has taken place, so long as that parent has final decision-making authority over extracurricular activities.

An important note, each issue regarding legal custody can be divided between the parties. So, for example, if one parent cares more about education than the other parent, then he or she could be the final decision-maker on school, and the other parent could be the final decision-maker on extracurricular activities, religious upbringing, or medical treatment.

Sole Legal Custody

Sole legal custody is difficult to achieve if both parents are involved in the child's life. In sole legal custody, only the custodial parent has the authority to make important decisions impacting the overall well-being of the parties' child.

The parent that does not have sole legal custody will be unable to select the school attended, serious medical treatment provided, or sports played by their child without permission from the sole custodial parent. However, the non-custodial parent can still take the child to the doctor or make less impactful or more urgent decisions without always conferring with the sole custodial parent.

Physical Custody

Physical custody determines which parent or guardian the child lives with. Physical custody is the type of custody most parents think of when considering or facing divorce. Physical custody concerns what parent the child spends overnights with throughout the year.

Types of Physical Custody

Joint Physical Custody

The child will spend a predetermined or close to equal amount of time with each parent throughout the school year and during summer and winter breaks with joint physical custody. The parties may deviate from the specific schedule by agreement; however, each parent is entitled to seek relief from the court when the other parent interferes with their physical custody time.

Most physical custody orders are a version of joint physical custody. However, there are multiple versions of joint physical custody impacting the amount of time a child spends with each parent and the specifics of the visitation schedule.

Sole Physical Custody

Sole physical custody is just what it sounds like: the child lives with one parent only. The other parent may have visitations with the child; however, the child will not have a substantial period of overnights with the non-custodial parent in sole physical custody.

Split Custody

Although it is considered unusual and rarely implemented, split custody is an option best suited for some families. In split custody, the couple has more than one child, and each parent is awarded primary custody of at least one of the children, with different visitation schedules for different children. Usually children will spend. Weekends and holidays together with one of their parents on an alternating basis.

Bird Nesting

Bird nesting is an unusual custody method in which the children remain in the marital home or family home full-time, and the parents rotate in and out of the family home on a specific schedule. This arrangement is sometimes used during divorce to ease the transition for the children; however, it is rarely used as a physical custody agreement or physical custody order once a divorce is finalized.

Where will the child sleep at night? What will the child's visitation schedule, if any, look like? When both parents are fit and proper parties to have custody of their children, it is almost always the case that both parents have some amount of physical custody over the children. Many courts presume joint physical custody if both parents exhibit that they can provide a proper and safe living environment for the children.

The issues related to legal custody, major life decisions for your child, and physical custody, such as where your child lives or sleeps at night, are often the most contentious in divorces involving minor children. Developing a game plan for what works for you, your children, and your soon-to-be former spouse assists you in planning your divorce and potentially assists in resolving your divorce early.

The Child Custody Process

In most Oklahoma divorce cases with children, one of the biggest fights is over what parent gets custody. Some couples facing divorce discuss the issue of child custody and reach an agreement; however, most cannot agree on all terms of child custody and litigate the issue of child custody. In this section, we examine the child custody process, and hopefully, you will gain insight into the process ahead in your divorce case. By understanding the process of a child custody case, you will be better prepared to face the road ahead in your child custody case or divorce with minor children.

How Is Child Custody Decided?

An agreement of the parties eventually decides most child custody cases, called a "settlement" or "agreed order." Oftentimes, it takes the parties many attempts or much back-and-forth to reach an agreement. In this process, your chosen divorce attorney or family law attorney must provide you with a clear understanding of the risks and rewards of fighting over child custody versus reaching an agreement.

One of the biggest benefits of an agreed child custody order is your control over the outcome. The earlier you identify to yourself and your attorney what you want the custody of your children to be, the easier the process is for you. In looking at the types of child custody and what each implies, you can begin to evaluate what matters most to you.

For some parents, having final decision-making authority is crucial. However, for other parents, it is crucial to spend a substantial amount of time with their children on a routine basis or to be with their children on specific days of the year. Whatever the issues that matter most to you, the earlier you can evaluate and determine the desired child custody arrangement and what you are willing to settle for in your child custody case, the better.

Temporary Orders in Child Custody

Early in many contested child custody cases, the parties appear for a temporary order hearing before the court. During the temporary order hearing, the parties, with the assistance of their attorney, present their evidence and arguments for their desired temporary custody order during the divorce.

Although these orders are temporary, it is very important to fight for the visitation schedule and temporary custody orders you want for your children. Oftentimes, the status quo or new normal established at this phase lasts for the rest of the divorce process and can even establish child custody arrangements after the divorce. Do not overlook the importance of this crucial phase of your divorce with minor children. By establishing the physical custody schedule that you want at this point, you increase the chance of it remaining in place beyond the final divorce order.

Guardian Ad Litem and Child Custody

In some contested child custody cases, an attorney is appointed by the court to represent the best interests of the child. These attorneys are called "guardian ad litem" (GAL). The GAL is supposed to be a neutral third party that evaluates the parents and the children on multiple bases to form a report to the court concerning the children's best interest for custody.

Selecting a specific GAL in your divorce with minor children or a contested child custody case is very important. GALs are people, and frequently they tend to lean towards one perspective or another; therefore, it is important to speak in detail with your chosen divorce attorney to identify and retain the GAL that is fair to you and your interests related to child custody.

Mediation in Child Custody

Most family law judges have more cases on their docket (meaning all the cases assigned to one specific judge) than the court has time to hear. Therefore, different systems have been put in place to assist parties in reaching a resolution without a lengthy trial before the court. Mediation is one of the most common of these tools in contested child custody cases or divorces with minor children.

Mediation in child custody cases is an opportunity for each party to appear with their attorney before a neutral, and often very experienced, family law attorney and present their case for the third-party mediator to evaluate. During and after mediation in a child custody case or divorce with minor children, the mediator gives their opinion on the likely outcome at trial, if the case proceeds to trial.

The mediator can discuss the law and its implications on the facts of the case at hand and makes recommendations for resolution to the parties. Often, the mediator may present a resolution between what each party wants in an attempt to find a middle ground that each party is willing to accept with finality. Again, an agreed resolution before a mediator provides certainty versus the unknown of a court order following trial.

Another benefit to considering mediation in a contested child custody case or contested divorce with children is that an agreement at mediation may be enforceable in court. Sometimes, a party has buyer's remorse following mediation and before a court order reflecting the agreement can be entered. In those cases, the party refuses to jointly petition for a court order to put into effect the agreement at mediation. However, your attorney can seek to have the court enforce the agreement at mediation, which may save you the pain, heartache, and money of the uncertainty of a contested divorce trial.

Child Custody Trial

In your divorce or child custody case with minor children, the family law judge schedules a trial if the parties do not reach an agreement. The family law judge has the authority and obligation to decide all unresolved issues in your divorce or child custody case at trial. Therefore, any issue the parties agree upon can be excluded from trial, which leaves only the unresolved matters for the court to decide in your divorce with minor children.

The family law court is required to consider certain elements in a contested child custody case or when custody is contested in a divorce. Contested child custody cases are typically determined based on what the court determines to be the child's best interest. This term or standard can seem all-encompassing and very daunting to parents facing divorce. However, it is intended to afford the court much room for interpretation so that it can achieve equity in deciding the physical and legal custody that is best for the children in the specific divorce before the court.

The outcome in a contested child custody matter may not be apparent to the parties or the court at the beginning of a custody battle. However, the court commonly uses the following factors in custody fights to help determine the custody arrangement that serves the best interest of the children:

- The relationship between the children and each parent.
- The physical and mental health of each parent and how, if any, health problems impact the parent's ability to provide care for the children.
- The potential for spousal or child abuse by each parent, including any past acts of abusive tendencies or instances of abuse.
- The criminal history and/or substance abuse history, if any, of each parent and other potentially harmful habits or behaviors of each parent.

- Each parent's ability to meet the needs of their children, including finances, home stability, living arrangements, safety of the environment, and the decision-making ability of each parent on behalf of their children.

When the court believes the children are mature enough, the court may inquire as to the children's preference on where to live. However, the weight, if any, given to the children's preference depends on the judge's propensity to listen to the children and the age of each child.

While the law may require the court to *consider* the preference of any child over a certain age (for example, 12 and over in Oklahoma), the court is not *bound* by the child's preference, and the court must determine whether the child is making an intelligent choice before considering the child's preference in determining child custody.

The Child Custody Order

After a contested child custody trial or divorce trial with minor children, the family law judge enters a binding custody order on the parties. The court's order decides legal and physical custody, including a custody plan detailing when children will be with each parent. Although the order is final in the family law court, a parent may file an appeal for a higher court to reconsider, and potentially overturn, a family law court judge's decision about legal custody, physical custody, and any other issues before the court.

After the passage of time (for example, a minimum of six months in Oklahoma) and upon showing a material change in circumstances, a party can seek to modify an existing court order regarding child custody. The party seeking the change must show that a "permanent, material, and substantial change in circumstances" has occurred between the court's custody order and the request to modify.

Can I Obtain Full Custody of My Children?

Parents have a duty of care for their children. Custody remains a bone of contention among separating parents. Parents who wish for full custody of their children must ask for it. However, the process may not be as simple as it sounds, especially if the other partner wants the same thing.

Custody battles can get messy; some parents use this as a last resort to hurt their partner. Family law courts usually prefer to award joint custody to parents. However, there are times when parents feel strongly about full custody, and they must work with an experienced family law lawyer to improve their chances of obtaining full custody.

Getting Full Custody

To get full custody, you'll need to file a motion before the appropriate family law court requesting full custody. The court will schedule at least one hearing on the matter after the motion. The number of hearings will depend on your reasons for requesting full custody and the other parent's response to the motion. Sometimes, both parents may agree to vest full custody in one parent; this happens in rare cases.

Sole Custody Disputes: What's Best for the Child?

While the parents battle for custody, the court is more concerned about the children and what's best for them. Parents living together practice joint custody; meaning many times, both parents are involved in decisions regarding the children's health, education, religion, and other important aspects. This relationship can be maintained even after a divorce has been finalized. Divorced parents can agree to joint custody arrangements, with living apart as the only difference. Courts often consider this to be the best approach to divorce and separation. Joint custody gives the children access to both parents and helps them form a lasting bond with each.

Under law, neither the father nor mother is considered a superior parent. Each parent is regarded as holding equal rights in making decisions regarding their child. However, in divorce, parents may push to have it all by requesting full custody and, as a result, sole decision-making authority.

To determine what is in the child's best interest, the court understands that each child and family is unique. Courts consider several factors in the buildup to a decision. A parent who wishes to obtain full custody must fully care for the child, physically, mentally, and emotionally. Before deciding, the court will look at the child's survival needs, including food, clothing, shelter, a stable home life, care, and love. The court will also consider the parent's emotional availability. There is a higher chance that the court will award primary custody to the more stable parent that can maintain a lasting relationship. To improve their chances, a parent seeking full custody must prove these elements and much more to the court.

If you are considering seeking full (i.e., sole physical and legal) custody, you should work with a skilled attorney to build the best case to support your request.

Child Support Considerations

Child support is a direct payment to the primary custodial parent from the other parent.

What Does Child Support Cover?

Child support is intended to cover at least the following basic needs of minor children: food, clothing, education, and housing. However, in many states, child support can be considered for other needs of minor children, such as medical care, childcare, transportation expenses, and extracurricular activities, as well as any expenses related to those needs. Some parents choose not to receive regular child support payments in exchange for the parent who owes child support being obligated to finance specific high-dollar expenses related to the child's needs. Because child support is a right of the child, it cannot be waived entirely. However, as previously stated, past and present child support may be waived.

Financial Benefit of More Overnight Visitations

In some states, the non-custodial parent can receive a shared parenting credit if the physical custody order gives them the right to more than a certain number of overnight visits in a year; for example, in Oklahoma, if the child is supposed to stay with the non-custodial parent for more than 120 overnight visits, the credit applies. When you qualify for the shared parenting credit, your child support obligation is reduced by a predetermined percentage.

However, you must be careful with the shared parenting credit because if you qualify but fail to achieve the specified number of overnight visits, the other parent can seek court relief to increase child support.

Because many parents spend substantial money directly supporting their children, it may be in your interest to reduce your child support. Suppose in your custody discussions, the number of overnight visits is already near the threshold to qualify for a shared parenting credit. In that case, it is in your interest to increase the number of nights per year to get to that threshold. For example, if in Oklahoma and discussing 2 per week or approximately 100 overnight visits, try to increase the number to 120. You will spend more time with your children **and** save money on child support.

Child Dependents and Conditions for Claiming

Claiming a child as a dependent is a great tax benefit, which you should not give up in divorce lightly. You should put protections in place, if possible, to protect your interest in claiming a child as a tax dependent. You can set conditions for a parent to be able to claim a child as a dependent for tax purposes. One common condition for claiming the child as a dependent for tax purposes is that the parent who is obligated to pay child support is current on their child support payments. Such a condition can be a useful tool for protecting your right to claim the child as a dependent for tax purposes while ensuring receipt of financial benefits. Even if there is no child support award, you can condition their ability to claim the child as a dependent on their compliance with other requirements in the divorce or child support order.

There are many non-standard agreements that can be reached to protect your financial interests related to child custody and child support. You should explore these options with a family law attorney or knowledgeable financial advisor.

Relocation

In the context of child custody, relocation refers to moving a child more than a predetermined number of miles from the child's residence when the custody order is entered.

Relocation of a parent or child is complex in a child custody case. Most child custody cases involving relocation are a result of one parent voluntarily moving. This section discusses such cases, leaving the topic of servicemembers to our special section on Military Divorce.

Relocation Statutes

State statutes on relocation typically contain multiple requirements a parent must meet, including providing notice to the other parent prior to relocation.

State family law typically presumes it is in the best interest of every child to have a strong, continuous relationship with both parents. Therefore, timely and meaningful notice must be provided to a former spouse or the other parent of a child prior to moving a child or children out of state. A party seeking to relocate with a child must notify the other parent or party with custody or visitation rights as soon as possible. State law may provide a minimum notice requirement; for example, in Oklahoma, notice is required at least sixty days prior to the relocation.

The non-relocating party or former spouse has the right to seek a court order to stop the relocating party from moving out of state with the child or children. At the hearing, the court decides whether the proposed move is being made in good faith or is an attempt to deprive a party of visitation or physical custody of their child or children.

Relocation Notice Requirement

The notice required before moving out of state with a child or children must include the specific information found in state law. These requirements may be difficult to meet when relocation occurs on short notice.

Among other things, the notice of the intent to relocate must typically include:

- The intended new address;
- The new mailing address, if different;
- The home telephone number, if known;
- The date of the intended move or proposed relocation;
- Specific reasons for the proposed relocation of the children; and
- Revised visitation or custody schedule.

The above list of information is based on Oklahoma statutes, and you will want to check your state law or consult an attorney prior to relocating out of state.

The relocation notice must also meet certain procedural requirements, including a minimum notice period before the proposed move (for example, 60 days). This period may be shortened if the parent planning to relocate could not reasonably have known earlier. Even then, a shorter minimum period is required (for ten days in advance in Oklahoma).

The notice requirement exists for so long as a party has a right to custody or visitation, and the relocating parent can be held in contempt of court if they do not comply with the notice requirement. Other consequences exist for failure to notify. Specifically, the family law court may consider failure to notify in deciding on modification of custody or visitation, and the relocating parent may be required to pay the other parent's attorney fees and court costs.

The relocation is legally allowed only if the party notified of relocation does not file an objection within a specified time after receiving notice of intent to relocation. For example, the time to object is 30 days in Oklahoma.

Process to Object to Relocation

A party must file an objection with the court to initiate an objection to relocation. It is crucial to act as soon as possible to avoid waiving the right to object, which expires within a short time after notice, as noted above. The party objecting is entitled to a hearing in court. At the hearing, a party may obtain an order requiring the other parent or custodian to return to the state or to return the child or children to the state or a contempt of court ruling for violating the relocation statute.

Whether you or your former spouse intend to move out of state, it is crucial to understand your obligations and rights to comply with your custody order and state law.

Custody and Support Modification Procedure

Child custody and child support orders are court orders that can be changed only by a new court order, known as a modified order. Even if you and your spouse agree to a change in terms, you must submit the agreement to a court for approval.

Motion to Modify

If you want to modify child custody or child support arrangements, you must first file a Motion to Modify with the court that issued the original order. This motion must contain certain information, including the parties seeking modification and the proposal for modifying custody, child support, legal custody, decision-making authority, or other changes being sought.

Summons

As with other court proceedings, the Summons is the formal notice to the former spouse that they must file a Response within a specified time (for example, twenty days in Oklahoma) or risk a default judgment. The summons must be served on the former spouse unless they waive service.

Response

The former spouse who did not file the Motion to Modify, the Respondent, should file a Response that identifies their position on the issues raised in the Motion to Modify. They may include a Counter Motion to Modify with their own requested changes.

No Automatic Temporary Injunctions During Modifications

As explained earlier, family courts issue Automatic Temporary Injunctions (ATIs) to protect the interests and assets of the parties during divorce proceedings. These ATIs are not, however, available in a Motion to Modify. That does not mean that the parties can do whatever they want; the court orders concerning custody and child support remain enforced unless and until the court issues a modification order.

No Additional Temporary Orders During Modifications

Similarly, the types of additional orders available during divorce proceedings, such as those covering possession of the marital home, alimony, and possession of specific assets, such as the family car, are not available in modification proceedings.

Motions

Although motions or applications for temporary orders are unavailable during a modification proceeding, other avenues are available to parties. Either party may submit a formal request, or "motion," to the family law judge for specific orders during the modification proceeding. Some of the most common motions involve requests for protective orders, restraining orders, and motions to compel discovery.

Hearings

Some issues must be resolved before the final modified order is issued, but the parties cannot resolve them by mutual agreement. In such cases, the family law court may hold a hearing to decide the outcome of issues those issues. A common issue litigated in contested custody modification is where the child will live and who will have what decision-making authority, or legal custody, for the child.

Discovery

Discovery in a motion to modify is the process that allows each party to submit requests to the other party for information, which in theory, allows both parties to learn more about the opposing party's case in the modification proceeding. To obtain this information, the parties may request documents or other physical evidence or ask questions of the other party in writing (interrogatory) or in person (depositions).

Mediation

The parties may be required to participate in nonbinding mediation before the court schedules a contested hearing or bench trial on a motion to modify. Mediation allows both parties to present their side of the case to a neutral third-party, the mediator, who gives advice on what they think is reasonable or what they believe the trial judge would likely order in the modification hearing. The modification procedure or issues in the motion to modify, such as child custody, can be resolved if the parties reach an agreement during mediation.

Custody Trial

If mediation is unsuccessful, a trial on the motion to modify is the final hearing before the family law judge. Both parties present evidence, witnesses, financial records, and even expert witnesses in some cases. The family law judge listens to the parties and decides the outcome of all issues before the court, meaning those raised in the Motion to Modify and any Counter-Motion. A party may appeal for review of any issue decided against them. Otherwise, the parties must draft the necessary documents to enforce the court's decision.

Judgment

The final order is typically a modified Joint Custody Plan or Modification to the Divorce Decree. The final order of the court, whether agreed by the parties or decided by the judge at a contested modification trial, governs child custody, child support, and all other issues raised in the modification petition. Property and debt divisions are not subject to modification, absent duress, coercion, fraud, or misrepresentation,

SECTION 6: FINANCES IN DIVORCE

"John took the reins and provided us instant peace of mind. He was timely, respectful, transparent, very professional, honest and courteous. The service he provided was above and beyond our expectations. Can't believe professionals like him are around. Highly highly without reservations recommend him and his team."

Julia

Protecting Your Finances Before, During and After Divorce

Divorce cases can be stressful and complex. Most people facing divorce fail to prepare for the financial aspects of divorce. You can face financial ruin if you or your spouse make bad financial decisions during a divorce. The movies may have glammed up divorce, but people with real-life experiences know how financially tough the process can become. Finding your footing after a divorce depends on how well you plan your finances before and during the split. Knowing how to protect yourself financially is essential if you are considering taking this step or are already in the process. Below are some tips that help to protect your finances in divorce.

Protecting Your Finances Before You Get Married

It may be an uncomfortable conversation, but it is important to set boundaries with your future spouse before tying the knot. This is especially true if you have substantial assets to protect in the event of a divorce. These protections start before the marriage begins.

One way to do this is to keep property that you want to keep as separate property. Separate property is not divided. Separate property is owned by either spouse before marriage and not commingled after marriage. Commingling of property occurs when one spouse's separate property is combined/mixed with marital property during the marriage, thereby losing its independent status.

For example, if a wife owned stock in a company before the marriage and never commingled funds with her husband's funds once married, those stocks would remain hers upon divorce. Or at least her divorce attorney would have a good argument that they remain separate property.

Another way to protect your finances before marriage is a prenuptial agreement. This is a written agreement between you and your fiancé in which you both agree to certain conditions in the event of a divorce. Generally, prenuptial agreements keep finances and assets separate, define alimony obligations, protect business interests, and limit debt liability.

This agreement is powerful because it allows the parties to pick in advance what they are awarded. A court upholds the agreement if it is fair and reasonable and if the parties were honest in their disclosure of what they owned at the time of agreement. In other words, a spouse cannot trick the other into an agreement where the other spouse does not have knowledge of the extent of the other's assets r debts.

Protecting Your Finances During Marriage

Marital property is acquired with marital funds during marriage. Marital property can also begin as separate property, but the funds contributing to it were commingled. The safest way to separate marital property is not commingle the property, i.e. for one spouse to provide all maintenance and cover all expenses from non-marital funds.

Keeping records is also vital to protecting your assets during marriage. Make copies of marriage certificates, wills, deeds, account numbers, tax returns, and account statements for deposits, mortgages, credit cards, and marital loans.

Most of this is needed during a divorce anyway, but you can also offer it as proof that certain property has always been separate. Keeping clearly separate funds or accounts and not comingling assets that you bring into the marriage assists in defending your property interests.

Protecting Your Assets When Preparing for Divorce

Once the topic of divorce or separation is introduced, you will want to start preparing to protect your property interests. If you and your spouse are breaking up amicably, it is a good idea to try to agree on things you want to divide among yourselves before seeking a divorce.

Sometimes when both spouses are high-earning and have a lot of their own assets, they want to resolve these issues without court involvement. However, a word of caution: without the assistance of an experienced high asset divorce attorney, you may miss identifying and collecting your interests in marital property if your spouse attempts to hide or define it as separate property.

You should identify all your cash resources. Divorces, especially ones with substantial assets, can get expensive. Cash resources give you an idea of how much money you are willing to spend if the divorce becomes highly contested. Identify assets that you are not willing to give up or lose. Collecting all documents on all the finances and property in the marital estate is vital to success in a high asset divorce.

Another thing to do is identify and index joint accounts and separate accounts for both parties. Ensure that all records are up-to-date and review new account statements as they arrive. If a spouse withdraws money for something other than legitimate marital bills during divorce, the court can order that spouse to reimburse the joint account.

Also, open a bank account in your name only and start using that personal account, as opposed to the joint account. Ask your attorney for a reasonable amount of money to deposit from the joint account into your new personal account.

Establish Separation or Divorce Legally

Once the topic of divorce or legal separation has been decided, there is no point in delaying the inevitable. Taking the right steps to legally initiate the divorce process is the first step toward starting a new life. Filing for divorce or legal separation affects how the money made after this date is handled.

Your income during the divorce process may be protected as a separate asset if you take the proper steps to protect your financial assets during divorce. Otherwise, your financial assets may be considered marital property. For instance, if you have been separated for eight months before the divorce proceeding is filed, your income for those eight months is calculated as yours, not marital property. However, any payments made toward marital debt/obligations may benefit your spouse.

You may have to spend some funds to hire the right Oklahoma divorce attorney; however, the costs of hiring the right team to help you through your divorce pays huge dividends in your case.

Protecting Your Assets During Divorce

Once a divorce case is filed, the parties are expected to "maintain the status quo," which means they cannot participate in any extreme activity that they would not have engaged in if they were not getting divorced. Typically, this is reinforced by a temporary injunction or temporary order that manages what the parties can or cannot do during a divorce.

First, if you have not consulted with a lawyer, do so. An experienced divorce attorney can help you protect your assets at all stages. They can advise you on the best way to manage each of your assets and how to protect your investments and financial interests.

If there is not a prenuptial agreement to divide property, you need to address how you and your partner want to divide the assets. Otherwise, your divorce attorney needs to be prepared to protect your interests in court. You and your divorce attorney must identify and value your assets and liabilities.

Valuable Assets to Protect May Include:

- All real estate property, including houses and vacation homes
- Cars
- Bank accounts, joint and separate
- Stocks and bonds

- College funds and debts
- Income tax refunds
- Cash value of life insurance policy
- Retirement savings
- Loans that you have made to others
- Jewelry, artwork, and collectibles

What to Do After Your Divorce

After you obtain your divorce, you should modify or update your estate planning documents. Although your former spouse may be disinherited by operation of law at the time of your divorce being finalized, it is better to avoid the confusion and make your desires clear by creating new estate documents. An Oklahoma divorce attorney that handles high asset divorces can assist you in ensuring your wishes are reflected in new estate planning documents.

When you are married, many of your accounts have a beneficiary designation directed to your spouse. You must remove your former spouse as the beneficiary designation on these accounts at the appropriate time. When you fail to remove your ex-spouse as the designated beneficiary on accounts, such as life insurance, they will likely receive these funds, or your family will need to engage in highly contested litigation over these funds. In other words, address beneficiary designations as quickly as possible.

When the divorce court enters an Order for you to pay a portion or all the other parties' attorney fees, it will be enforceable. Fortunately, this is typically reserved for a prevailing party after the case is finalized in a separate contested proceeding. However, if you reach an agreement that one party will pay attorney fees, or if the court enters this Order, you may be held in contempt if you fail to pay.

It is important to include language in your Decree regarding the responsibility of parties related to payment of attorney fees.

High Income Earners Should Have a Different Strategy than Low Income Earners When Facing Divorce

Divorce financial analysts may recommend not taking all the items you originally requested in your divorce because higher income may result in disqualification from beneficial tax deductions. Personal exemptions for high-income earners become unavailable at certain milestones if you file your taxes as single. It is wise to speak to a financial analyst to determine the best course of action for your financial situation and options to mitigate your tax consequences in divorce.

Get a Clear Understanding of Your Property

An essential step to understanding how divorce will impact your finances is to understand exactly what property will be affected by divorce.

Dividing marital assets and marital properties is not only a mathematical transaction. Identifying property, determining its origin, and negotiating the division of property is a complex process that boils down to three steps: 1) determine the nature of the asset, 2) determine the asset's value, and 3) divide marital property. Each step is likely to be contentious.

This section explains how to determine what property is in play and who owns it. In the divorce proceeding, each party is expected to be forthright and honest in providing financial information to the court. With full information, the court is better able to make the right decision about who gets what.

Definition of Property

The term "property" does not simply refer to land in family law. Instead, it includes many types of assets: real estate, cars, boats, firearms, furniture, jewelry, bank accounts, retirement accounts, business interests, and most things in which a person can have an "ownership interest," including pets, such as, yes, "the dog."

Marital Property versus Separate Property

State laws make a distinction between "Marital Property" and "Separate Property." Marital property is any property jointly acquired while a couple is married. Separate property encompasses all property acquired by only one spouse, either before, during, or after marriage. Separate property is not subject to division by the divorce court.

Property received as a "Gift" is considered *separate if the gift is only for* one spouse. However, if the gift is made to the couple, it may be marital property. Property received as an *inheritance is separate property.* When one spouse conveys part of the property to the other spouse, it becomes marital property. Courts may consider property *obtained in exchange for or from the proceeds of separate property* as separate property as well. Basically, if the acquisition of a specific item of property is *unrelated to the marriage, it may be considered separate property.*

Asset Documentation

Document your assets, period. Make copies of all bank transactions and statements, including retirement statements. If you have investments, make copies of your investment statements, and keep them with your attorney. If you suspect your spouse may be trying to hide some of their assets, it is best to inform your attorney, who can take proactive steps to uncover those hidden assets and finances.

Hiding Assets Does Not Work

You are violating the law if you hide assets in a divorce proceeding. When you hide assets during your divorce, and it is discovered, the court can sanction you, including potentially losing money through those financial sanctions. To protect yourself and your property during divorce, it is best to declare assets honestly.

The Discovery Process Will Help Uncover All Assets

Although both parties involved in the divorce are expected to be honest, this isn't always the case. The discovery process allows each party to work on uncovering all assets. A wide range of tools is available during this process, and you should take to your family law attorney to decide how to engage in proper discovery for your case.

When you suspect that your spouse may be mischaracterizing assets or hiding significant assets, you may want to work with a forensic accountant or other financial expert to carefully follow the paper trail and uncover undisclosed assets.

Retaining Financial Experts Is an Investment

When financial assets and interests are at stake, it is crucial that you work with an experienced family law and divorce attorney to protect your financial interests and future. In some cases, it is necessary to retain additional expert advice or financial analysis to ensure that all accounts are identified and closed or transferred properly to protect you from future tax implications or negative credit consequences. Although it will likely be expensive to work with experts to assist in dealing with your divorce's financial records and division, it is an important investment to make for your future.

Considerations in Hiring a Private Investigator or Forensic Accountant in Divorce

Many people facing divorce do not want to spend the money to hire a private investigator or forensic accountant in divorce. Forensic accountants can assist you in obtaining accurate information on all the financial issues in your marriage and divorce, which may save you far more money than the expense.

Identify Your Most Valuable Asset

Many people mistakenly believe their home is their most valuable asset; however, in many cases, one party's retirement account or pension is the most valuable asset. Although your retirement account may not be accessible at the time of divorce, its future value may have substantial dividends. Using a Qualified Domestic Relation Order, you can divide your portion of your former spouse's retirement account or pension without being required to follow up decades from now.

Separate Debts

Lenders, especially credit card companies, are all about their money and do not care about your divorce. You remain liable if your spouse builds up a huge debt on a jointly owned account. Leaving your marriage with no debt is much better than having debts to pay months or even years after the divorce's finalization. Now is the time to address the debt. If you have the money to clear the debt, do so. However, if you can't, it is best to divide the debt into two parts, transfer it to individual accounts, and close the jointly held account.

Request Your Credit Report and Monitor Your Financial Activities

Whether or not you held a joint account with your spouse, having an idea of what your finances are like is essential. Going into a divorce, requesting a copy of your credit report is essential.

How Property is Divided in Divorce

It can be easy for one spouse to decide what they definitely don't want to fight for the separation of property. In any divorce settlement, it's important to decide what YOU want before deciding what you're willing to give up.

Once property is characterized as marital or separate property, the next step is determining the property's value and then an appropriate division. Some property is more complex to value and divide. This section explains some of the key issues that arise with division of property.

"Division of Property" in State Divorce Law

State divorce law determines the division of property in a divorce if there is a dispute. There are two property classifications in American divorce laws: community property and equitable distribution.

In community property states, income, assets, and debts are divided equally. There are only nine (9) community property states as of 2022: Arizona, California, Idaho, Louisiana, Nevada, New Mexico, Texas, and Washington.

However, the other forty-nine (49) states, including Oklahoma, are equitable distribution states, which is better for retaining your assets. Knowing how equitable distribution impacts your divorce can help you prepare for the process of dividing assets in divorce.

A Refresher on Types of Property

Separate Property

Essentially, marital property is the presumed status of property. Property must fall within a specific category to qualify as separate property, so your spouse isn't afforded a marital interest in the property. To qualify as separate property, one of the following criteria must exist:

- Property owned by the spouse prior to marriage;
- Gifts to one spouse, not both spouses;
- Legal settlements obtained on behalf of only one spouse; and
- Inheritance granted to only one spouse.

Marital Property

Property not meeting one of the separate property criteria above is marital property, and both spouses are entitled to a marital share. Marital property is subject to division in a divorce. The equitable division of property approach trumps legal title.

Marital property may include cars, houses, bank accounts, retirement accounts, 401(k), IRAs, and many other forms of assets, property, and accounts.

Equitable Distribution

In an "Equitable Distribution" state, family law courts divide marital property between spouses in a "just and reasonable" way.

Marital property can be divided by a settlement agreement, at mediation, or at trial by the court. When the court determines the division of property in divorce, the division is not necessarily equal; rather, it is equitable. Multiple factors go into this analysis. In a divorce settlement decided by the parties, "equitable" is whatever the parties agree is fair. Only in cases in which the parties cannot decide on a fair distribution of marital or separate property will the court determine property division.

Family law judges have wide discretion in determining the division of property as separate or marital property in divorce proceedings. The only statutory guidance is that the division be "just and reasonable." It is important to note "just and reasonable" often does not mean equal.

Factors Used to Determine Just and Reasonable Division of Property

Family law judges attempt to divide marital property fairly and reasonably, and they have wide discretion in determining what is considered separate or marital property during the divorce process. Judges consider multiple factors, including the contributions made by each party to the household.

Family law judges can consider the efforts of the respective parties during the marriage in divorce proceedings. Even in divorce cases where one party is a homemaker that does not work outside the home, the court considers the party's responsibilities to the home as a relevant contribution to accumulated assets.

The fact that one spouse earns more than the other *does not justify an unequal distribution* of the marital estate. In other words, a working spouse is not entitled to a greater portion of the marital estate than the stay-at-home spouse, because both contributed, presumptively, equally to preserving the marital union.

In a no-fault divorce state, family law judges do not look at the fault of either party when considering the fair share in property division.

To complete an equitable division of the marital estate, a family law judge must consider not only those assets accumulated during the marriage but also the debts of each spouse. Sometimes, only one or two items of property are left to divide after subtracting debts from assets. When neither spouse can afford to pay property division alimony (a financial payment to the other spouse to divide the asset's value without selling it), the trial court can order that the asset be sold. The money from the sale can then be divided.

In litigated property division, the court determines whether:

- specific items of property are marital property or separate property;
- the value of marital assets;
- the parties' contributions to the assets in the marriage;
- sacrifices made during the marriage by one party to support the other party in their professional or other endeavors;
- involvement in raising the children, if any;
- marital efforts that contributed to the increase in value of an otherwise item of separate property; and
- other variables either point towards marital efforts increasing the value of an asset or not playing a role in the asset's value.

Courts determine a monetary value for every marital asset, going back to the date of separation or when the Petitioner filed the petition for divorce, and distribute all marital assets based on the established value.

Process for Division of Financial Marital Property

Separating houses, vehicles, and material objects can be straightforward if the parties agree on what is most important to each; however, financial assets are usually more complicated to divide. It is more complicated to define the value of extended assets, such as investment portfolios, retirement accounts, 401(k), IRAs, and other investment accounts for equitable division of these assets. Assets not yet realized, such as an IRA or retirement account that has not matured, create substantial complications for determining value, and may require hiring an expert.

Severance of Jointly Held Property or Title

When the spouses own property jointly, family law judges are tasked with dividing the property by vesting title to the property in one of the spouses. To do this justly, the court typically awards the entire property to one spouse and awards property of similar value or division alimony to the other spouse.

Who Gets the House?

You or your spouse may be personally attached to your family home; however, it is a financial investment whether you view it that way or not. You or your spouse may not want to sell the family home; however, one of you will need financial compensation if the other spouse keeps the marital home. The equity in the marital home, compared to the balance owed on the mortgage, is an important consideration in determining the amount and type of debt you want to carry.

If neither party can afford to stay in the marital home after the dissolution of marriage, the court may force a sale and divide the proceeds accordingly.

Who Gets the Dogs?

Pets are considered personal property, not children, despite how many people feel about their pets. The parties can either reach an agreement for the division of personal property, including the dog or other family pets; however, if the parties cannot agree, then the divorce court judge or a mediator may decide the particulars of dividing individual assets, including "man's best friend."

Modification Is Typically Barred

The property division component of a divorce decree is a final judgment that cannot be modified. Except in fraud cases, the decree bars a claim by either party to the property of the other spouse. The property division portion of the divorce decree survives death and is binding on both spouses' estates.

It is important to tell your chosen family law attorney early in the proceedings of any property item that has significant meaning to you! Your divorce attorney can assist you in forming a plan to keep that asset in the divorce.

Retirement Accounts, Not as Simple as Account Balance

Retirement accounts or pensions often account for the largest asset jointly held by either party in a divorce. Considering the amount of time and effort it has taken you to build those accounts, you may not want to share those funds with your spouse.

Unfortunately, unless you have specified otherwise in a prenuptial agreement, family law judges consider retirement benefits earned during marriage to be marital property. Alternatives may exist to avoid the division of retirement accounts and pensions. In this section, we discuss common solutions.

Protecting Separate Property Portion

You should note that pension and retirement division during a divorce aren't automatic. The portion the spouse can request depends on the length of the marriage and how long the account has existed. The value of an account prior to marriage is generally separate property in divorce proceedings and should be protected.

Qualified Domestic Relations Orders

Retirement benefits can be allocated to a spouse during a divorce utilizing a Qualified Domestic Relations Order (QDRO).

The distribution of retirement benefits is very important because it can have financial impacts on both spouses. Determining the value of a retirement account is difficult in most circumstances. Deferred taxes must be paid at some point on many retirement accounts, which can greatly reduce the true value of a retirement account. Liquidating a retirement account early comes with serious tax consequences in most circumstances;

therefore, avoid early withdrawal and use tools like a Qualified Domestic Relations Order (QDRO) to avoid these tax consequences.

A QDRO, pronounced "Quadro," is a family law court order used in divorce cases to give a portion of a party's retirement benefit to a requesting spouse. As part of the divorce settlement, the family law court order instructs a retirement plan administrator to give a certain portion of the beneficiary's retirement benefits to their spouse.

Who Is Eligible for a Qualified Domestic Relations Order?

A QDRO is defined in the Internal Revenue Code by the IRS and the Employee Retirement Income Security Act (ERISA). QDROs apply to those retirement plans covered by the Internal Revenue Code and ERISA unless specifically excluded. Importantly, among those plans excluded from ERISA are governmental retirement plans. Thus, the retirement plans of state and municipal employees, federal employees, teachers, and police officers do not include a QDRO to divide retirement plans between spouses during a legal separation or divorce. However, many states have passed laws allowing these plans to be divided in a way that mirrors a QDRO, even though the court orders have different names.

Additionally, every retirement plan has its own set of rules. For example, some plans offer survivor benefits, while others do not. Some plans allow a spouse to collect a lump sum distribution upon retirement or to choose an annuity payment for a fixed term or life, while other plans only allow one course of action.

Tax Implications of a Qualified Domestic Relations Order

QDROs are particularly complex due to the tax implications of such a family law court Order. A spouse must pay taxes immediately if they receive retirement benefits outright or if they deposit the money into a bank account. However, if the funds are deposited into a separate retirement account, taxes are not due until the money is withdrawn years later.

The IRS considers a Qualified Domestic Relations Order (QDRO) a judgment, decree, or Order concerning a retirement plan. Additionally, the IRS requires reporting the benefits received from any QDRO to the IRS as if you are a plan participant and receiving a proportionate share of the financial benefit of the account. You are allowed, without penalty by the IRS, to roll any payment from a QDRO plan into another retirement account, for example, an individual retirement account or IRA.

How does a QDRO benefit me?

Using a QDRO allows you to receive benefits of a retirement plan that you are legally entitled to receive. Simply having a divorce decree that states you are entitled to a portion of a retirement account is insufficient to provide you the funds from a retirement account. You need a QDRO to transfer all or a portion of the benefits from a retirement plan to anyone other than the plan participant. However, a QDRO cannot distribute a portion of every retirement account. QDRO is only applicable to qualified retirement plans, covered by the ERISA.

The types of qualified retirement plans under ERISA are defined contribution plans and defined benefit plans. You cannot divide military retirement, government pension, or an IRA by use of a QDRO. Different laws and regulations govern these assets. For instance, you do not need a QDRO to divide an IRA or SEP account.

The effects and procedures of a QDRO can be incredibly complicated and may vary depending on the terms of a retirement plan and whether an employer is a private company or a government agency. It is essential to consult an experienced family law attorney when trying to divide assets held in a retirement account.

Types of Retirement Accounts to Consider in Divorce

Retirement Accounts come in many forms, and different rules apply to the division or early collection of each type of retirement benefit. When facing divorce and division of retirement benefits, it is vital to understand the laws and regulations governing the retirement benefits you are entitled to in your divorce.

The majority of retirement benefit accounts fall into one of the following categories:

- Pensions
- Deferred Compensation Accounts
- 401(k) Account
- Individual Retirement Accounts (IRA)
- Simplified Employee Pension (SEP) Plan
- Military Retirement and Government Retirement Accounts

This is not an exhaustive list; however, most retirement accounts fall under one of these large categories.

Defined Contribution Plan

The most popular or most common defined contribution plan is the 401(k). These plans are rather simple to value as they have a current cash value or balance at any given time. The court or parties can divide a 401(k) or defined contribution plan by multiple methods. Many people facing division of retirement in divorce elect to roll defined contribution plan benefits into another retirement account to avoid the tax consequences of early withdrawal. However, you are not required to do so and may withdraw immediately if you choose.

Most retirement plans are subject to a 10% tax penalty or more for early withdrawal before age 59.5. The benefit of using a QDRO is this tax penalty is usually avoidable, as the QDRO is exempt from this penalty. However, any funds you withdraw or receive from the 401(k) are subject to income taxes.

Defined Benefit Plans

Pension plans are the most common defined benefit plan. These plans are more difficult to determine the current value for than defined contribution plans, such as a 401(k). This is because these plans guarantee a specific amount of money per month at retirement. Additionally, any growth in value of a defined benefit plan or pension before or after a divorce is not marital property, so it is not subject to division. Therefore, if you were only married for a portion of the time your pension value was growing, it is very difficult to determine your spouse's share of the benefit.

Fortunately, defined benefit plans can be divided by a QDRO, just like a defined contribution plan. Typically, the method of division of a defined benefit plan takes one of the following three forms:

1) Cash Out: The former spouse receives a lump sum as settlement for the present value of the defined benefit plan;
2) Deferred Division: Present value is not determined for the defined benefit plan, and each spouse receives a defined share or percentage of the plan's benefits when the plan is paid; or
3) Reservation of Jurisdiction: The court retains jurisdiction or authority to divide the benefits at a later date.

Additionally, working with the pension plan administrator for each account is important to establish survivor benefits. You can preserve your rights to your entire pension plan if your ex-spouse predeceases your retirement.

Individual Retirement Account (IRA)

The IRA account is rather simple to divide in a divorce. The portion of the account each spouse receives is typically rolled into another retirement account without suffering transfer penalties or tax consequences. However, if you or your spouse elect to spend your share of the proceeds of the IRA, that party is subjected to a tax penalty of 10% and potentially other account penalties for premature withdrawal of funds.

You can speak to your IRA account coordinator or IRA custodian regarding the specific information or documentation needed to execute a division of the IRA; however, in most cases, a divorce decree, which lays out the division of the account, is sufficient for the account custodian to divide the account.

Can I Get Alimony?

Whether a spouse is entitled to alimony depends on the divorce law of the state where you file for divorce. Most states support alimony payment and use various factors to determine whether it is necessary and what amount is appropriate in each divorce case.

What Is Alimony?

Support alimony is money provided from the more financially independent spouse to the less financially independent spouse after divorce to reduce the immediate impact of the change in finances. Alimony is need-based, and the initial burden to prove the need for alimony is on the spouse seeking alimony.

Factors in Determining Alimony

The two primary factors for determining alimony are:

1) the needs of the party receiving alimony, and
2) the ability of the other spouse to pay

To evaluate these two primary factors, courts look at multiple other factors:

- Demonstrated need during the post-divorce economic readjustment period
- The parties' station in life
- The length of the marriage and the ages of the spouses
- The earning capacity of the parties, as well as their physical condition and financial means
- The accustomed style of living of the parties
- Evidence of a spouse's own income-producing capacity and the time needed to make the post-divorce transition for self-support

Taxes in Divorce

Taxes During Divorce

Taxes are a part of life in America, and being married comes with many tax benefits. Years of marriage and dependable income allow for accurate preparations for federal and state taxes. Married couples get in the groove of compiling brokerage statements, W-2, receipts, and other materials for taxes. Many of our clients have accountants that assist in this process each year, including CPAs, which allows you to prepare for how much money you must collect to prepare for your expected taxes. How you pay taxes and what you must give to the IRS during divorce are a couple of the most common questions we are asked regarding divorce and taxes.

Many of our clients worry about not accurately reporting income for state and federal taxes during divorce. Horror stories are common concerning tax liabilities during divorce. What happens if my spouse doesn't pay any taxes? Will I be liable for my spouse's failure to pay the IRS? Ignorance of tax laws during a divorce is not a defense. It could cost you large penalties or even impact your retirement. There are plenty of reasons to be worried about taxes during divorce; however, there are solutions to each of these concerns.

Some tax consequences are dormant for years. Consider a lake house, or other asset, which appreciates year after year; without proper accounting, you could face a giant capital gains tax that was unexpected.

The year you go through divorce will be unlike any other year for tax purposes. It will be complicated, but you can be prepared. Sit down with your Certified Public Accountant. Additionally, consider the assistance of a forensic accountant to give you advice for your specific situation.

Our divorce lawyers can explain important concepts, such as "commingling," "transmutation," and others relevant to taxes and divorce.

We cannot give you tax advice, but an experienced CPA can. Don't worry. We can introduce you to some great CPAs, if you do not have an existing relationship with any. In the meantime, review IRS Publication 504, the IRS's "Divorced or Separated Individuals" guide to preparing taxes.

Look Out for Hidden Tax Consequences of Divorce

Looking out for hidden tax consequences and obligations during divorce is important. When you transfer a stock that has increased in value during divorce, you are on the hook for the tax for capital gains. When you transfer or receive real estate, stocks, bonds, or other taxable gains, you are on the hook to pay taxes on these assets unless your former spouse is responsible for these expenses.

Financial Considerations in a High Net Worth Divorce

Divorce is very rarely a simple process. And while divorce rates have been falling in recent years, reports reveal that the COVID-19 crisis triggered a near 21% increase in divorce agreements this past year. Divorce proceedings are a difficult and complicated process, regardless of the couple's situation. However, one of the most common issues in a relationship usually boils down to finances; more often than not, this carries over into the divorce.

There are a few considerations to keep in mind when filing for a divorce with high financial assets. Here are some of the things that are very important to consider:

Length of Divorce

There are complexities involved with having more assets during a divorce. Time determines the cost, and while most divorces take anywhere between a few months to a year, it may take longer for individuals with a high net worth.

Splitting Taxable and Non-Taxable Assets

During a high-asset divorce, you must be cautious in dividing retirement savings, 401(k) accounts, IRAs, Roth IRAs, and other investments. Substantial tax penalties lurk behind division or liquidation of investment accounts before retirement or maturation. It is important to divide assets fairly, not liquidate them, as much as possible.

Tax Issues and Custody Disputes

Fighting for child custody is one of the most significant factors that affect divorce. Working out how to share a house and children is difficult enough in a divorce, but amplifying this with multiple homes, plots of land, businesses, and assets makes the matter much more complicated. Computing your taxes may change depending on your financial situation during the divorce.

Managing Spending

Divorces are expensive. Unfortunately, some believe that the more money they spend on the divorce, the more favorable the outcome. However, the court often views this behavior negatively, particularly for those with considerable wealth. Regulate your expenditures until the divorce is finalized.

Understanding these financial considerations may give you a better chance at achieving the best outcome.

SECTION 7: A MILITARY DIVORCE GUIDE

Outstanding law firm, their experience with military law and the civilian sector is the best I have worked with. Professional office, amazing staff and overall just amazing people that will go the distance for their clients. They care about their people and in getting the best outcome they can for their clients. Recommend as the #1 office in OKC and Edmond.

Ben

There's no denying it: divorce is one of the worst things to deal with in life. Nobody ever gets married intending to divorce. Everybody wants their fairy tale wedding and happily ever after story. Unfortunately, sometimes people grow apart. While the divorce process is always emotionally charged and legally complex, the military divorce process is even more complicated and has many factors beyond a civilian divorce.

Military Divorce is Complex

Military divorces are especially complex due to the issues related to military life and the protections afforded to servicemembers. By divorcing a servicemember, the civilian spouse is putting themselves at risk of losing many of the benefits they may depend on. If the servicemember is still in the military, they may be stationed elsewhere or have to address their work duties while the divorce is ongoing. You can reduce your stress and save time and money by understanding the military divorce process.

The first step we take when you decide you're ready for a divorce is to determine the best state to file for divorce. It's vital to remember that the state where you were married does not affect the divorce proceedings, only the state where you are stationed, live, or domicile with intent to live permanently.

Military Divorce versus Civilian Divorce

For those in the military, the divorce process is much more convoluted than the civilian process. Service obligations, including deployment, may complicate the military divorce process; however, the process is the same as a civil divorce process. The greatest difference between military and civilian divorce is the interests at stake, which are governed by military regulations and federal law. Things like child custody, alimony, property, child support, and debt division can all differ from a conventional divorce.

Complicating Factors

Divorcing a military servicemember can be very complex, or it can be relatively straightforward. It all depends on your unique situation and whether there are any complicating factors. For example, if there are assets that both parties want, you might have to fight for your rights. Similarly, having young children makes finding a viable arrangement more challenging.

If you and your spouse are considering filing for divorce from abroad, you should make sure that a US court will recognize this. It's always best to file directly in the US since this might make enforcement easier. Family law governing proper jurisdiction to hear a divorce action, as it relates to military servicemembers, allows for the filing of your divorce in the state the service member is currently stationed, the state in which the service member claims legal residency or domicile, and the state in which the other spouse claims legal residency or domicile. The term "domicile" means the place or jurisdiction in which a person intends to remain permanently, which can be contested by the other party.

Military divorce is a highly specialized area of family law. The benefits you may or may not be entitled to in a military divorce are precious. Seeking the best possible outcome in your military divorce is complex and will generally require the help and support of an experienced military family law attorney. Experience matters when you are facing divorce as a servicemember or servicemember's spouse. It is important to know that the family law attorney you hire is versed in military family law.

Military Divorce Laws: State and Federal

Unlike a divorce involving two non-service members, military members and their spouses that face divorce must consider federal laws and regulations.

Understanding the governing laws and regulations for the specific issue or issues in your military divorce is important. Having a good understanding of these laws prepares you to seek the desired outcome for the issues in your military divorce.

In short, state family law governs the aspects of divorce common to everyone, and federal laws and regulations govern the aspects of divorce specific to a military divorce. State law dictates the process for seeking child custody, visitation, child support, division of most property and debts, and support alimony, all the major aspects of a divorce, except certain aspects of property. Specifically, state law does not govern the division of military-specific assets. Federal laws and regulations dictate the division of military retirement, Survivor Benefit Plans, military medical benefits, and various other military specific interests in divorce. Additionally, federal laws provide service members with certain protections that may affect some of the procedural aspects of divorce.

Federal and military-related laws and regulations change regularly, and new developments can affect the outcome of your case. Experienced military divorce attorneys have a wide network of industry contacts, so they always stay well-versed in regulation changes and amendments to existing rules

This section summarizes key aspects of the federal laws that will likely be relevant in your divorce if you or your soon-to-be ex-spouse are a servicemember.

Servicemember Rights in Military Divorce

The Service Members Civil Relief Act (SCRA) provides numerous protections to servicemembers facing the complete span of civil legal processes, including in military divorce involving active-duty servicemembers.

In a divorce when one party, the Petitioner, files a divorce and serves their spouse with the Petition for Dissolution of Marriage, the other spouse, the Respondent, is required to file an answer in the divorce case. However, in the case of an active-duty servicemember, if the servicemember is unable to respond or appear due to a service obligation, they are protected from a default divorce decree, or other negative consequences, in the military divorce process pursuant to the protections provided under the SCRA.

The SCRA specifically provides for "stay" or postponement of any civil court or administrative court proceeding, including a divorce proceeding, if the service member presents evidence that they could not respond in the statutory time based on a duty obligation.

A servicemember is qualified for the multiple SCRA protections, including a stay of civilian legal proceedings, if performing military service, which is defined under the SCRA as follows:

- Full-time active-duty members of the five military branches (Army, Navy, Air Force, Marine Corps and Coast Guard);
- Reservists on federal active duty; and
- Members of the National Guard on federal orders for a period over 30 days.

These protections take effect immediately upon receiving military orders for reservists, including National Guard soldiers on active duty.

This protection does not allow a servicemember at their duty station simply to avoid participation in the divorce process. Rather, it is a protection for servicemembers on specific orders, including national disaster response, overseas military duty, and other types of orders that remove them from their home station.

The SCRA is perfect for servicemembers, but it can be frustrating if you're a military spouse because it can significantly lengthen the time to finish your divorce from a service member. Under this act, the court cannot issue any permanent legal decisions until the military service member can be physically present.

SCRA Application to Reservists

The SCRA generally protects a spouse in a military divorce that is or will be on active duty in the immediate future. These protections apply to both National Guard servicemembers and reservists. The family law court postpones or suspends substantive hearings in your military divorce if your service obligation qualifies for the protections afforded under the SCRA. State laws or court decisions may limit the application of the SCRA and other military protections to specific service obligations or orders that reservists are called to serve under.

What Happens If an Overseas Spouse Never Answers Divorce?

In most cases, if your spouse fails to answer your petition for divorce by the statutory deadline, you may seek a "default divorce," or a divorce from the court, without input from your spouse. When a court grants a default divorce, you typically receive exactly what you wanted in the divorce. The other party, your former spouse, is obligated by court order to abide by the terms of the divorce decree you presented to the court.

However, in the case of a military divorce, the court must stay proceedings until the military servicemember is able to return and answer your divorce petition. Though in some circumstances, the court appoints a lawyer to represent the servicemember's interests. In most cases, the court stays, entering a final order or default divorce, as servicemembers can return home on leave or at the conclusion of their overseas tour to respond to the divorce proceeding.

Servicemembers and Appearing in Court

A servicemember may waive the protections under the SCRA and their entry of appearance and opportunity to file an answer to the divorce petition. In many cases, the servicemember may agree with the terms of divorce offered by the non-servicemember spouse and benefit from finalizing the divorce before deployment.

Legal Assistance for a Military Spouses Facing Divorce

Generally, the military views divorce as a private civil matter to be addressed by a civilian court. However, military spouses have access to military legal assistance services at no cost through installation of legal assistance offices. In a divorce, a servicemember and dependent spouse need separate attorneys to advise them to ensure both parties receive independent and confidential advice and avoid any conflicts of interest. The legal assistance office is prohibited from representing you in your divorce and likely does not know the family law in the state you are stationed. It is important to hire an experienced military divorce attorney where your case is pending.

Rights of Former Spouses in Military Divorce

You now know that the SCRA protects active military servicemembers from the court issuing judgments against them if they're overseas. However, there are also laws designed to help former spouses of military members. The Uniformed Services Former Spouse Protection Act (USFSPA) is a federal law that gives benefits to former spouses of those in the military.

The USFSPA does not directly award a part of the military benefits to the servicemember's spouse; however, it authorizes family law judges in Oklahoma to divide the retirement benefits accrued during the marriage according to the state law.

In the case of a military divorce, divorcing spouses may choose to negotiate a settlement in the place of a judge's ruling; however, military servicemembers are well served to do whatever they can to protect their military retirement by substituting the marital share for other assets provided to their spouse. We discuss military retirement in more detail later in this section.

Uniform Deployed Parents Custody and Visitation Act

The Uniform Deployed Parents Custody and Visitation Act (UDPCVA) is a national response to address custody and visitation issues for servicemembers. The UDPCVA is intended to provide additional protections beyond the SCRA discussed above. It focuses on protecting servicemembers from losing their rights to custody or visitation, regardless of service obligation. The UDPCVA is not a federal law but a model act intended to guide state legislators in adopting state laws that protect servicemembers uniformly across the country. To date, ten states have adopted state laws enacting the provisions of the UDPCVA, and others are pending enactment.

Benefits for Former Military Spouses

The Uniform Services Former Spouse Protection Act is a federal law that provides military benefits to a former spouse of a military servicemember.

Any former military spouse who has not remarried and qualifies for the 20/20/20 rule, which we describe in more detail later, receives the following benefits:

- Military medical benefits, including healthcare coverage under TRICARE;
- Installation access, including the benefits of the commissary, exchange, and other services that are only on post; and
- Access to the Army Morale, Welfare, and Recreation (MWR) programs.

Child Support against Servicemembers

All military servicemembers are responsible for supporting their children and their spouse if they are still married. This requirement includes separated spouses if a divorce decree has not been filed. You may contact your military servicemember's chain of command if they refuse to provide you and your children with Basic Allowance for Housing (BAH) and support. It is a service requirement and actionable under military justice, if you fail to provide for your dependents. The military takes the matter seriously if your spouse refuses to do so. An experienced military divorce attorney can put appropriate pressure on the party directly, or through their command structure, if the servicemember spouse violates their obligations.

Military Divorce Process

Where to File a Military Divorce

One of the most significant considerations with a military-related divorce is where to file. Being in the military often means moving around a lot. The state where you file is crucial because it establishes jurisdiction. Without it, the divorce won't be valid, which is why it's crucial to meet at least one of these three points to meet the requirements regarding jurisdiction:

1) You can file where the military spouse is a legal resident
2) You can also file where the military spouse lives
3) You could also file in a different state upon which both parties agree

Filing Overseas

The location where you file is crucial for another reason. If you and your spouse lived overseas when you filed, the US courts might not recognize your foreign divorce as legal. If you or your spouse has already filed overseas, it's crucial to contact a US military divorce lawyer for a consultation about how to best proceed in your particular situation.

Did you know that if you're overseas and you divorce, your family and their belongings can be brought back home stateside on the government's dime before the tour of duty ends? An experienced military divorce lawyer can help you apply for this assistance.

Pausing a Military Divorce Proceeding

The SCRA is a federal law that allows the servicemember to obtain a stay of proceedings, much like a continuance. A stay on proceedings allows you to stop the military divorce case from moving forward for a time. When military duty requires you to be outside of the jurisdiction or unable to appear in court, the SCRA and your military divorce attorney can stay the proceedings for a time.

The SCRA provides a stay of military divorce proceedings only when needed. Service members may face consequences for abusing this privilege. An initial SCRA stay of military divorce proceedings requires a notice to the court hearing the case. The statement must indicate the servicemember's military duties preventing them from currently participating in the military divorce. Additionally, the statement to the court must be accompanied by a statement from the servicemember's commanding officer, indicating their military duties prevent them from appearing and answering the military divorce action, and their leave is not granted.

Subsequent SCRA stays may be granted with sufficient and specific information provided by you or your military divorce attorney. It is important you or your military divorce attorney articulate how your response to the lawsuit or absence from duty/training negatively impacts your military training or service obligation. Courts deny SCRA stays, sanction, or punish servicemembers who mischaracterize their inability to appear in court for a military divorce action.

Civilian Spouses and Military Benefits

Divorce is always an emotional and complex process, but it can be even more daunting for civilian spouses of someone in military service. They might have been benefitting from housing, healthcare, and a pension related to their spouse's service; so, starting on their own is financially challenging. When going through a military divorce, it's worth researching which assets or benefits you might be able to keep and which ones you may have to give up.

In the case of a military divorce, the parties are bound by the federal regulations that govern the division of military retirement and other benefits. For example, the benefits the civilian spouse is entitled to depend on how long they have been married, how long the servicemember has been active in the military, and how many years these overlapped. In general, you have many rights if you have been married for a long time, especially once the marriage exceeds twenty years. This section provides a closer look at how divorce affects military benefits.

Rights of Civilian Spouses in a Military Divorce

When you married your military spouse, you gained access to many benefits related to their service. The exact nature and extent of these depend on the type of service they are performing, but most people have healthcare, housing, and a pension. Now that you are contemplating divorce, you might be worried about which ones you can retain and which ones you'll have to give up.

Every situation is different, and the length of service and the marriage significantly affect the outcome. If in doubt, you should request a consultation with a lawyer and figure out where you stand.

The 20/20/20 Rule

Some civilian spouses can keep most of their benefits, such as medical care, commissary, exchange, and theater privileges. This is true as long as they don't remarry, which causes them to lose access to all these services. Although the Army Morale, Welfare, and Recreation program may sound very generous, it only applies to specific situations. You can benefit from it if you meet the criteria of the 20/20/20 rule.

When a former military spouse qualifies for the benefits under the 20/20/20 rule, they receive access to the maximum benefits for former spouses. To qualify for the 20/20/20 rule, a former military spouse must meet each of the following criteria:

- The former military spouse was married to the service member for at least twenty years before the dissolution of marriage or divorce;
- The military member performed at least twenty years of creditable military service towards the determination of retirement pay; however, the military member does not have to be retired from active duty; and
- Finally, the former military spouse must have been married to the military service member for at least twenty years of overlapping military credible service and marriage.

There is no requirement that the servicemember be currently retired, and this rule applies whether or not they are still working.

The 20/20/15 Rule

If you weren't married to your military spouse for the full twenty years of their service, you may still gain access to some benefits. Specifically, you can get TRICARE medical coverage if the service member completed twenty years of service, you were married to them for twenty years, and at least fifteen of those years overlap. Unfortunately, you won't be able to claim many of the other benefits offered to those who meet the 20/20/20 criteria.

Housing and Moving Costs

BAH stands for Basic Allowance for Housing. The Basic Allowance for Housing in the US is determined by zip code or geography. The servicemember's military duty location, pay grade, and dependency status determine the BAH total.

Each military branch requires that military members pay a separated spouse a monthly sum to live on; however, a civilian family court order may remove or increase this requirement. In the army, the amount due is equal to BAH-II or the national BAH prior to adjustment for specific duty station.

BAH payments cease upon divorce or a family law court order terminating this entitlement. Former military spouses are not entitled to BAH; however, during separation and the course of the divorce process, unless an existing court order states otherwise, the military servicemember is required to provide BAH to their spouse. Action can be taken through the servicemember's chain of command to ensure these benefits are provided.

As long as the military divorce is ongoing, you should be able to keep your housing. However, you should start making alternative arrangements once the divorce is close to being final. Installation family housing is only for service members and their spouses, so you must vacate the home within thirty days of your servicemember spouse's move-out date.

A highly qualified attorney can help you figure out what to do in this situation. They determine when exactly you may be asked to leave and help you find a new arrangement. If you have a problem or are unable to find housing on your own, your lawyer can refer you to organizations that can assist you as you make this transition.

Veteran Affairs Disability Compensation

Servicemembers' disability payments from the Department of Veteran Affairs are not divisible marital assets. This is still the case if the military servicemember waives some retirement to receive VA disability compensation. This action is commonly referred to as a "VA waiver." The non-servicemember spouse should protect their interest in the military divorce by requiring substitute compensation if the servicemember elects to take this action. Failure to implement this protection results in a reduction in the compensation to the non-servicemember in the military divorce.

An indemnification agreement can protect a former spouse from a VA waiver. For a non-military spouse, a VA waiver can greatly reduce the benefits received from the Department of Veterans Affairs or DFAS. It is essential to have a waiver clause in the military divorce decree or agreement, requiring the servicemember to repay any amount lost to the non-servicemember spouse if disability compensation is taken from the pension.

Military Medical Benefits after Divorce

Healthcare is another vital asset to consider in a military divorce. TRICARE and the 20/20/20 rule provide some of the best healthcare coverage in our country at little to no cost, if you are eligible. Unfortunately, military medical benefits are not a divisible marital asset. TRICARE and military medical benefits are created by right if the former military spouse qualifies under the statutory requirements.

Military divorce court orders don't impact the right to receive TRICARE. In fact, a military divorce decree that denies the right to military medical benefits typically isn't honored by the Department of Defense because it's an invalid order. The converse of this is true: if the divorce decree states a former military spouse is entitled to TRICARE, and they are not statutorily entitled, the federal government denies military medical benefits because it's an invalid court order.

Continued Health Care Benefit Program

Upon military divorce, the former military spouse is entitled to the Continued Health Care Benefit Program (CHCBP), the TRICARE equivalent of COBRA. This entitlement lasts three years. Suppose the former military spouse remains unmarried and was awarded a portion of the military retirement or Survivor Benefit Plan as part of the military divorce. In that case, the former spouse is entitled to remain on CHCBP for the rest of their life.

Unfortunately, CHCBP is expensive. In 2019, the plan costs $1,453 per quarter for an individual, or $484 per month. Therefore, although this is a right worth considering, oftentimes, there are less expensive health care coverage plans available in the private sector.

Post-9/11 GI Bill and Former Spouses

The Post-9/11 GI Bill is a very valuable military benefit. It can provide tuition payments, monthly housing allowance, and a stipend for books. In fact, in 2019, the Post-9/11 GI Bill provided roughly $160,000 in benefits for someone seeking a four-year college degree.

Additionally, this benefit is not only for the servicemember but can be transferred to a spouse or children if certain eligibility requirements are met. Going through a military divorce does not terminate access to these benefits. One's status as a GI Bill beneficiary is transferable to a non-servicemember if they meet the other criteria. Therefore, a former spouse may continue to receive Post-9/11 GI Bill benefits if the parties agree, preferably with an agreed order in the divorce decree.

Post-9/11 GI Bill benefits are not divisible in a military divorce. Federal law prohibits the division of Post-9/11 GI Bill benefits in a divorce. Servicemembers may agree to allow a former spouse to use the benefits of the GI Bill; however, the servicemember is not required to provide these benefits.

One benefit of providing GI Bill benefits to a former spouse is the possible impact on child support and spousal support. GI Bill benefits can be considered income for calculating spousal support and child support. The monthly stipend is considered income, for instance, valued at approximately $1,500 (dependent upon the school's location and the cost of living there). However, book stipends and tuition assistance provided under the GI Bill cannot be calculated as income.

Military ID Cards for Children after Divorce

Military dependent children under the age of ten are not issued military ID cards; however, in a military divorce, there is an exception to this rule. AFI 36-3036, Para. 4-3, states that children of any age that do not live with the sponsor, i.e. military service member, will be issued a military ID card. To obtain an ID card for a child, you simply have to apply by completing and submitting a DD Form 1172-2.

Although a military member's former spouse is typically not entitled to the benefits of base access, their children are entitled to these benefits. Therefore, a non-military parent may access military instillations with their child holding a military ID or Common Access Card (CAC).

Legal Separation and Impact on Military Benefits

The Department of Defense treats legally separated military spouses as married to the military member for purposes of entitlement to military benefits. AFI 36-3036, Table 8.3 states the following in the joint regulation concerning legal separations in the military: "Do not terminate a spouse when an interlocutory divorce or legal separation occurs."

Additionally, a "former spouse" includes only a spouse that has gone through divorce, dissolution of marriage, or an annulment; therefore, legal separation does not make the list. Therefore, legally separated spouses are entitled to important resources provided to the servicemember, such as a military ID card or CAC, base access, commissary benefits, and access to all other military benefits provided to a military spouse.

However, legally separated spouses do not continue to accrue retirement benefits upon entry of the divorce decree. The period of legal separation does not count towards the period of military retirement benefits, nor the 20/20/20 or 20/20/15 time frame analysis for medical services for the former military spouse.

Military Retirement: What You Should Know

As a serving member of the armed forces, you are expected to make sacrifices as part of the job. However, these sacrifices earn you a chance to enjoy some benefits–one of which is military retirement.

Military retirement is valuable to you and your spouse as you build a life together and plan for the future. However, when the issue of divorce is brought up, you need to know how this affects you, your spouse, and the substantial military retirement you have accrued over the years.

Certainly, in all divorce cases, both parties are expected to part with certain valuables, be it property, debt, money, or others. The service-related benefits earned as a member of the armed forces are not excluded in military divorce cases.

If you have earned a military retirement during your marriage, it is common for the military retirement to be regarded as a part of the marital estate. This means it is subject to division. There are different approaches to how military retirement is divided, depending on state family law, and, more importantly, federal regulations concerning military retirement.

Depending on state law, the court may be required to treat military disposable retired pay as part of the marital assets, which means that it is divisible as a marital asset during a military divorce. The Department of Defense allows servicemembers to waive their military retirement and receive disability pay as an offset, which reduces the amount of their disposable retired pay, and consequently, the former spouse's retirement award in the divorce.

Unwary former spouses and inexperienced lawyers not versed in military benefits have been led to believe decrees granting a percentage of a servicemember's retirement were to be taken literally. However, the unilateral actions of the servicemember after the divorce can reduce the spouse's share to literally zero if adequate protections are not included in the divorce decree.

The 10-Year Rule

Servicemembers often believe that their marriage is expected to have lasted no less than ten years for their spouse to be entitled to a share of their military pension and retirement. On the contrary, this isn't a standing rule. A former military spouse is entitled to their marital share based on the years of marriage that overlap with military service towards retirement.

However, a servicemember's divorced spouse will receive direct payments from the Department of Defense if:

○ The marriage lasted at least ten years, and
○ The service member earned a military retirement for at least ten years during the marriage.

After ten years of service and ten years of marriage that overlap, the Department of Defense collects the retirement for the divorced spouse. The spouse has to make the proper applications for retired pay promptly, and while many practitioners rely solely on a divorce decree, it is better to have a separate order requiring direct payments to the spouse. This avoids confusion on the anniversary date of retirement when the decree and the client's perception of events do not coincide.

Should the spouse not qualify for enforcement of the retirement division by the government due to not being married to the servicemember for ten years, then that spouse must resort to collecting amounts due pursuant to the divorce in the same fashion as any debt. In this regard, the decree should state that the servicemember is ultimately responsible for any payment not made by the government beginning on the date of retirement. On many occasions, the servicemember does not make a timely application for retirement pay, or the government does not process the retirement in a timely fashion.

The Frozen Benefit Rule

Due to the new Frozen Benefit Rule, the National Defense Authorization Act (NDAA) has seriously reduced the claims available to a servicemember's former spouse in a divorce action. A servicemember's former spouse cannot benefit from promotions or other benefits to the servicemember after divorce.

Regardless of the parties' agreement in a military divorce; DFAS only pay based on the NDAA 2017 that calculates at the date of divorce. Specific and precise calculations apply to full-time servicemembers. The system for the Army Reserves and National Guard is even more complex. Retirement points and other factors must be considered, including the pay charge, to determine the high three.

Unfortunately, military retirement calculations that do not meet the DFAS requirements or calculations aren't enforced, which is non-negotiable. It is crucial to retain experienced military divorce counsel to assist you with your divorce if you or your spouse is a servicemember.

Can Military Retired Pay Be Garnished?

Military retired pay can be garnished. This can be done in line with requirements like child support or awarded amounts in spousal support. It is important to note that such a court-ordered requirement does not consider the marriage's length.

How Does a Pension Buyout Work?

You or your military divorce attorney can negotiate an exchange or buyout to compensate for the value of your share of military pension or retirement. Even a marriage that only lasts a few years may result in thousands of dollars of retirement compensation for the non-military member.

The servicemember spouse must pay equivalent compensation if they don't divide their military pension. As the non-military member spouse, you or your military divorce attorney must negotiate a fair trade. Ensure your military divorce attorney does a calculation that is fair to you.

Other Retirement Plans

The military offers a defined benefit pension plan to every servicemember serving twenty years of credible service. The military servicemember, and potentially the former military spouse, receives a monthly payment upon retirement, based on the servicemember's years of service, basic pay, and the retirement multiplier.

Historically, the multiplier for military retirement has been 2.5% multiplied by years of service. The easiest example includes twenty years of military service, which means 50% of high-three basic pay during retirement. This equation is the legacy retirement plan in the military. However, for new members and members who selected the Blended Retirement System, the multiplier is now 2% multiplied by years of service and the enhanced Thrift Savings Plan (TSP), which is now available.

Military retirement is very often a servicemember's most valuable asset. Some individuals have a military retirement worth hundreds of thousands of dollars on the low end. Alternatively, military members who retire at an elevated rank may be entitled to a military retirement worth over a million dollars -yes, more than $1,000,000! The value of these military retirement accounts makes them the most valuable asset accrued during the course of many military marriages.

Military retirement is a marital asset subject to division in a divorce proceeding, even if not vested at the time of military divorce. There are few caveats to the rule that a former military spouse is entitled to a portion of a servicemember's military retirement, even military marriages that only lasted a year or two.

The following are two crucial rules from the military and DFAS to consider in military divorce:

1. DFAS pays the former military spouse directly if the spouse had at least ten years of marriage that overlapped military service of their former spouse. The military retirement is an asset that is divisible at divorce, with less than ten years of overlapping marriage and military service; however, the military retiree is required to send payments directly to the former spouse each month; and

2. Payment of military retirement does not begin until the military servicemember retires. When a military servicemember dies, the Survivor Benefit Plan takes effect, which must be considered and protected by the former military spouse, or these benefits can be lost as well.

Thrift Savings Plan (TSP)

The military TSP has been around for a very long time. TSP is a defined contribution plan, similar to the civilian 401(k) plan that many businesses offer. The new Blended Retirement System provides matching funds from the military and partial replacement of the traditional military pension described in the previous section.

TSP is another valuable divisible asset in a military divorce. The former spouse is entitled to roll over their share into a qualified account, such as a Roth IRA, for tax and other benefits.

Survivor Benefit Plan (SBP)

Some divorce attorneys or servicemembers wrongly believe a surviving former spouse automatically receives the Survivor Benefit Plan. A military divorce settlement or divorce decree should specify who receives the SBP. Typically, this is awarded to the non-military spouse, especially if the marriage lasted for a substantial period of the military service. In some cases, a former spouse forfeits the SBP for another benefit, such as life insurance, which allows the servicemember to retain the benefit for a future spouse.

SBP coverage provides the non-military spouse 55% of the servicemember's base military pension for the rest of their life, which is a huge benefit to a non-servicemember. Without SBP, a surviving spouse receives no military pension or military retirement compensation beyond the servicemember's death. Without a court order concerning SBP, submitted to DFAS for military recording, it is the same as no agreement or court order. A military divorce attorney can help you ensure the recording and receipt of these benefits.

SBP Deadlines

You must submit the SBP court order to DFAS within the necessary time frame to receive the benefits. You must meet one of two SBP deadlines.

One deadline applies if the servicemember submits the court order, which is one year after entering the military divorce decree. The other deadline applies to the non-servicemember spouse submitting the court order for SBP coverage. When a non-servicemember spouse submits the SBP coverage order, it must be within one year of the court order, not the military divorce decree. The non-servicemember's DFAS request must include a "deemed election" request letter. The order must specify "former spouse" coverage; naming the spouse is not enough for SBP beneficiary. Your chosen military divorce attorney must be familiar with this rule and ensure it is followed to protect your benefits.

Restrictions on the SBP

The SBP cannot be divided. SBP can be waived, but it cannot be divided between multiple spouses, for example, your current and former spouse.

SBP coverage is not available when the former spouse marries before age 55; however, it can be reinstated if that person's new spouse dies or the marriage ends in divorce or annulment.

DFAS won't distribute SBP premiums between the parties. SBP premiums come "off the top" by law. They are deducted from gross pay to determine the divisible retirement income. The premium for SBP coverage is 6.5% of the selected base amount. This can be the servicemember's entire retirement pay. The court order must specify the base amount, or DFAS elects the full retired pay as the default. To protect against this, your military family law attorney must change the selection to the lower base amount for the SBP.

Too many times a soldier would walk into my office and inform me, "my spouse can't get any of my retirement; we haven't been married ten years." This fallacy still exists today, and nothing could be further from the truth. There are numerous ways to explain, but to focus on clarity, I will hone this down to the obvious.

There are many more nuances to a military retirement, including the Survivor Benefit Plan, Death and Indemnity Compensation, disability payment offsets, and numerous other events that can, and most likely will reduce your military retirement unless you protect yourself against these occurrences. I highly recommend hiring an attorney who has experience in these matters to protect yourself against drastic reductions in the military retirement benefit that you did not expect at the time of the divorce.

Spousal and Child Support

Every military servicemember is required to support their underage children and former spouse. There are policies to protect your rights, and you should find out which ones apply to the type of service your spouse was in. This is true even if there isn't an agreement or court order. A great divorce lawyer will be able to help you research this so that you don't lose out on valuable benefits.

Considering that this type of support is temporary, you need a court order for a more permanent support agreement. This is where your attorney's service proves invaluable, as they help you navigate the ins and outs of alimony and child support laws.

Military Child Custody Issues

Custody can be challenging for any family to work out, but it's even worse for people in the military, who often move around the country or even the world. You must figure out how to balance your children's need for stability with the importance of seeing their servicemember parent regularly.

Despite their job, the military employee has a right to see their children, and a suitable agreement must be worked out. In every case, your attorney attempts to find the optimal solution for the children. This often means shared custody, which allows them to grow up while maintaining a relationship with both parents. Servicemembers in military child custody cases, whether a military divorce or legal separation, battle over which parent their child should live with or have physical custody most of the time.

To navigate these challenges and help you find the best solution for the children involved, you should always employ the services of an experienced attorney. Check that they have worked with similar families before and are aware of the unique challenges that being in the military brings.

Many military custody disputes can be resolved prior to trial or through mediation; however, some military custody cases must be litigated in contested child custody trials. An experienced child custody attorney provides insight and guidance on many military family law issues, including:

- Child custody arrangements to meet the unique geographic challenges servicemembers face, from permanent-change-of station (PCS) moves, active-duty tours, and other service-related travel;
- Child support considerations for servicemembers and their unique and varied forms of compensation; and
- Your rights and protections associated with being a servicemember facing child custody or divorce issues while deployed or on orders away from home.

Regardless of whether you are a servicemember or the other parent is a servicemember, state law typically requires family law judges to consider the "best interest of the child" in deciding child custody.

Deployment and Relocation

Active-duty parents have it hard since deployment and relocation often make things even more challenging. In fact, deployment or relocation harmed past cases concerning custodial rights for divorcing military servicemembers. Currently, the court places the most stock in the child's best interests. However, this is another place where the SCRA can benefit you if you're in active service. If you're currently deployed overseas, it can help delay proceedings until you can be physically present.

Relocation Statutes and Servicemembers

To address the growing problem of the negative effects of relocation statutes on servicemembers, some states hav enacted laws (such as the Oklahoma Deployed Parents Custody and Visitation Act (ODPCVA)) to protect the rights of servicemember parents and their children in custody disputes. These laws seek to preserve the relationship between servicemember parents and their children during periods when a servicemember parent would be absent because of military service. They protect the rights of deployed servicemembers parents and their children in the following ways:

- Ensuring that child custody arrangements in place before they deploy will be reinstated post deployment; and
- Designating a person with a close relationship with the child, including stepparents, siblings, and grandparents, to exercise the deployed parent's visitation rights during deployment.

For example, in Oklahoma, when a parent is deployed and seeks relief under the ODPCV, the deploying parent has a right to transfer their visitation rights to a stepparent, a designated family member, or another designated individual. Within the ODPCVA, there is a rebuttable presumption that it is in the child's best interest for a stepparent, designated family member, or another designated person to exercise the deployed parent's custodial rights and duties.

Continuing with the example of Oklahoma, the ODPCVA provides protections to both parents and guardians with child custody matters during deployment. To qualify under the ODPCVA, a servicemember parent must show the following:

- They are a deploying parent; and

- Their mandatory leave qualifies as deployment under the statutory definition.

Working with a competent military divorce lawyer can help you more easily navigate this stressful process. They continuously alert you to important upcoming events, so you can be fully prepared for what's coming. As a result, you won't risk missing critical deadlines or making costly mistakes.

SECTION 8: TRENCHES OF DIVORCE LITIGATION

TRENCHES OF DIVORCE

"Everyone at this firm is outstanding! Very Professional and Respectful People! From the very beginning they treated me with Respect and took my case serious! The outcome for me was better than I ever expected!!"

Kenneth

Divorce Discovery Process

Divorces are a type of civil lawsuit; therefore, the general guidance/rules of civil procedure apply to divorce cases in Oklahoma. This is important to keep in mind, as having the right legal team in your divorce assists you in capitalizing on the rules of civil procedure. One of the most important tools of civil procedure in a divorce case is discovery. The discovery process is a tool in which each party can request information from the other party, and they are required to answer all questions under oath.

The divorce discovery process is an investigative period in which both parties involved gather information from the other party. At this stage, each party aims to gather as much valuable information about their case as possible. The discovery process is a precursor to settlement or trial proceedings.

Both parties involved in the divorce case are bound by state divorce law and civil procedure law, which outlines the scope of information that can be gathered and requested. For example, the Oklahoma discovery code provides the following specific provisions at Oklahoma Statutes Title 12 § 3226 (B)(1)(a), states:

> Parties may obtain discovery regarding any matter, not privileged, which is relevant to the subject matter involved in the pending action, whether it relates to the claim or defense of the party seeking discovery or to the claim or defense of any other party, including the existence, description, nature, custody, condition, and location of any documents, electronically stored information or other tangible things and the identity and location of persons knowing any discoverable matter. It is not a ground for objection that the information sought will be inadmissible at the trial if the information sought appears reasonably calculated to discover admissible evidence.

The Types of Discovery

There are many tools that fall under the discovery process. Although the most appropriate discovery tools vary based on the issues of your specific divorce case, the tools themselves remain the same across all civil cases, including divorce. Below are the primary methods of discovery divorce cases:

- Deposition upon written questions
- Deposition upon oral examination
- Request for production
- Interrogatories
- Request for Admission

The rest of this section is a brief synopsis of the discovery tools detailed above. We hope this information allows you to begin thinking about how to use these tools in your divorce case.

Deposition

A deposition is a question-and-answer meeting, similar to a witness testifying in court. A court reporter is present to type every single word, including both the questions and answers in the case. Additionally, the witness/party deposed is sworn to tell the truth. Failure to testify truthfully in a deposition may subject the witness to the penalty of perjury.

In the proper setting, a divorce deposition can assist you and your lawyer in exposing information the other party may not want out in the open, as well as provide an opportunity to practice asking the party questions under oath before trial in your divorce case. The following forms of discovery allow the other party thirty days and the advice of counsel in responding to every question or request; however, in a deposition, the person under oath must think on their feet and answer questions with limited or no assistance from counsel.

It is important to retain an experienced divorce attorney with experience in trial and depositions if you face a deposition in your divorce case. You can assist yourself by reviewing documents and records in your divorce, as well as thinking about any bad information in your personal life or the divorce process and how you want to address questions or topics of conversation that you are not excited about discussing. In many instances, depositions help to settle a divorce case.

Request for Production (RFP)

This request is aimed to compel the other party to produce certain documents in their possession or that they can easily obtain. The periods and limits described here are consistent with Oklahoma civil procedure, which broadly resembles other state law. You will want to consult an attorney for specifics.

The response to a request for production is expected to be provided within a thirty-day window. However, the respondent may be granted an extension period from receiving the discovery requests.

Each party involved in the divorce case is limited to thirty requests for production unless additional requests by the court are granted, which is rarely granted.

To submit a request to inspect an item of evidence, the initiating party has to meet the requirement prescribed by law. For example, Oklahoma Statute Title 12 § 3233 (B)(3) requires:

– That the request will contain specific information about the item demanded for inspection.

– That the request will specify a reasonable time, place, and how the document is to be inspected

– That the request states clearly the form or forms that electronically stored information may be produced.

Interrogatories

These are questions prepared by one party and presented to the other party, and that the responding party is required to answer under oath. Again, the periods and limits described here are consistent with Oklahoma civil procedure, which broadly resembles other state law. You will want to consult an attorney for specifics.

Replies to interrogations are expected in thirty days, or the other party may seek a request to compel responses by seeking court assistance. During the divorce discovery process, each party is limited to thirty interrogations unless certain circumstances demand an excess of the prescribed limit, after permission by the court.

For example, to request additional interrogatories in Oklahoma, the initiating party must follow the statutory procedure as contained in Oklahoma Statute Title 12 § 3233 (A).

> No further interrogatories will be served unless authorized by the court. If counsel for a party believes that more than thirty interrogatories are necessary, he shall consult with opposing counsel promptly and attempt to reach a written stipulation as to a reasonable number of additional interrogatories. Counsels are expected to comply with this requirement in good faith. In the event a written stipulation cannot be agreed upon, the party seeking to submit such additional interrogatories shall file a motion with the court (1) showing that counsel has conferred in good faith, but sincere attempts to resolve the issue have been unavailing, (2) showing reasons establishing good cause for their use, and (3) setting forth the proposed additional interrogatories.

Request for Admission (RFA)

These are true or false statements, similar to interrogatories, which one party prepares for the other party. Again, the periods and limits described here are consistent with Oklahoma civil procedure, which broadly resembles other state law. You will want to consult an attorney for specifics.

There is limit of thirty Requests for Admission for each party in the divorce case. Parties who wish to exceed this limit must follow the set of rules of the Court in order to seek additional Requests for Admissions. The Requests must be answered within thirty days of the date the request is made to the other party as dictated by Statutes Title 12 § 3236 (A), which states:

> The matter is admitted unless, within thirty (30) days after service of the request, or within such shorter or longer time as the court may allow, the party to whom the request is directed serves upon the party requesting the admission a written answer or objection addressed to the matter, signed by the party or by his attorney, but unless the court shortens the time, a defendant shall not be required to serve answers or objections before the expiration of forty-five (45) days after service of the summons and petition upon him.

To answer a Request for Admission, the receiving party can either admit, deny, or provide no answer due to the invalidity of the objection. When a party fails to answer a request for admission, the other party may seek to have the request "deemed admitted," meaning the party admits the requested admission by failing to respond.

Conclusion on Divorce Discovery

Many procedural and litigation tools exist in the divorce process. The discovery tools explained above are some of the most powerful tools to seek information and potential settlement avenues in your divorce case. With an experienced divorce attorney or divorce litigation team, you will be able to uncover much information about the other party in your divorce case, and either prepare for trial with knowledge of the facts and issues in your case or seek a settlement in your interests.

Alternative Dispute Resolution in Divorce

Alternative Dispute Resolution (ADR) is a means to solve legal issues outside a court setting. Litigating, family law, and personal injury cases can be expensive, burdensome, and lengthy, but ADR presents a streamlined and cost-conscious opportunity for the parties to avoid court and still solve their problems. Additionally, where courts are structured and follow certain rules, parties can have more flexibility in an ADR setting to set their own schedules and rules between parties.

Only 2%–3% of cases are settled in court—the other 97%–98% are settled out of court using one of these mechanisms. ADR is widely used because it can be used in multiple settings. Parties can write dispute resolution clauses into their contracts, the courts can order it, or parties can agree to do it themselves.

Selecting the Appropriate Method

There are multiple methods available to settle a legal dispute out of court, but it can be tricky to determine which method is best for your case. For this reason, it is important to talk to your attorney and determine which ADR method gives you the best outcome in your case.

The best method may depend upon your personal needs and the nature of the dispute; for instance, personal injury litigation requires a different type of ADR than a divorce case with minor children. Important factors in determining whether arbitration, mediation, or litigation is appropriate for your case include:

- Whether to handle the dispute in a private or public setting

- Whether an informal setting is more advantageous

- How flexible you would like the rules to be

- How much time and money you have to handle the case

- Whether or not you want personal control over the dispute outcome

- Who the opposing party is in relation to yourself

Sometimes, the most appropriate place for a dispute is the courtroom but participating in ADR allows parties the option to take more control over the legal process. Talk with your family lawyer about participation in different ADR methods to determine how to get the most value out of your case.

Arbitration

What Is Arbitration?

Arbitration is a process where a neutral third party, called an "arbitrator," hears arguments and evidence from both parties and decides the issue's outcome. It is a voluntary process, but both parties must agree to arbitration before they can do it; parties are not forced into participating in arbitration in most cases.

Arbitration has many advantages besides being less expensive and quicker than a contested trial. One of the most important advantages is that it generally releases the parties from the formalities of a courtroom setting, particularly regarding the rules of evidence. Parties can still present evidence and make arguments, but the parties can essentially make their own rules.

Additionally, many parties choose arbitration in family law cases because it is private, meaning the issues in your case are not available in the public record. This differs from family law litigation, as sometimes litigation results in parties' private information being brought out in court or in public.

Another advantage to arbitration is that parties can decide who their arbitrator is, and whether the arbitrator's final decision is binding. In binding arbitration, parties agree to accept the arbitrator's decision and generally give up their right to appeal that decision, for example, the decision of the arbitrator in a personal injury case is binding. This is effective for parties who just want the issue solved and do not want there to be any continuation. Nonbinding arbitration is especially powerful because it means that the parties may request a trial if they do not agree with the arbitrator's decision—effectively giving them a second chance if their first shot doesn't hit a bullseye.

Mediation

What Is Mediation?

Mediation is another kind of ADR that consists of negotiations assisted by a neutral party to facilitate a voluntary, mutually acceptable agreement. In mediation, the third party does not participate by deciding the outcome, but by helping the parties reach a decision themselves. The mediator assists in identifying issues, exploring possible bases for agreement, discussing the consequences of not resolving the dispute, and encouraging the parties to compromise where necessary.

If the parties have a close relationship, such as parents trying to reach a child custody agreement, they may choose mediation because it promotes communication and cooperation, and preserving their relationship is important. When parents do not choose mediation on their own, the court can also require them to participate in mediation but does not require that they come to an agreement. The ability of these parties to reach their own agreement can set an important precedent that they can reach agreements on their own and may prevent further litigation in future disputes.

Parties may also choose mediation because it is informal and flexible. Since the parties are negotiating the result of their dispute, they are not limited by court formalities and have the most control over the outcome. Additionally, similar to arbitration, mediation is private and confidential, which avoids public disclosure of any intimate, embarrassing, or otherwise private information of the parties. What is said or offered in mediation cannot be held against the parties in Court, including at trial.

Should You Mediate Your Divorce?

In family law cases, mediation allows both parties to meet with a neutral third party, typically a very experienced family law attorney, and present your case as if you were at trial. Experienced family law attorneys have participated in many mediations, dealing with various issues. By working with the right family law attorney who will help you select the best mediator for your divorce, you stand the greatest chance of a settlement with a positive financial and legal outcome.

Getting your divorce settled with a positive outcome is very important. For one, if you and your spouse are able to settle your divorce without going to trial, you control the outcome of your divorce. In mediation, the parties must agree to reach a settlement. Alternatively, if you do not agree in mediation, the family law judge over your case decides all unresolved issues.

When you and your experienced divorce attorney present your case to a mediator, you receive a forecast of what may happen if your case proceeds to trial. Insight into a contested divorce trial is one of the greatest benefits of mediation. The following are four important considerations in divorce mediation:

4 Considerations for Divorce Mediation

1. Systematized Discussions

Divorce mediation typically proceeds in a very organized fashion, with the mediator taking equal time to hear and respond to both sides of your divorce. Divorce mediation typically begins with the mediator speaking to both sides separately about the process for mediation. Next, the mediator takes a substantial amount of time to meet with one party and their divorce attorney to try to understand that party's position on the issues in divorce. After the first in-depth meeting with one side, the mediator meets with the other party and their divorce attorney.

The mediator expects you and/or your divorce attorney to be prepared to speak in depth about your finances, assets, debts, and goals for every issue in your divorce. You and your divorce attorney should prepare a marital balance sheet that details all relevant financial information for you and your spouse and a proposal for what you want on every issue in your case. The divorce mediator should not allow you to disparage your spouse or vice versa. Mediation is not the court of public opinion. You are paying for the valuable time of the divorce mediator and your divorce attorney to discuss the key issues in your divorce, not why you are divorcing your spouse.

2. Professional Guidance

Mediation is an intelligent negotiation between the parties through the guidance and experience of the divorce mediator. Throughout the course of your divorce mediation, you receive guidance from your divorce attorney, as well as the mediator, on what the law and rules of court dictate on different issues in your case, as well as what may or may not happen on individual issues if you have a divorce trial.

Divorce mediators with experience in divorce litigation advise you on the best case, worst case, and likely outcomes of the contested issues in your divorce. You will be better prepared to negotiate your divorce and reach a resolution at mediation if you have an in-depth discussion with your divorce lawyer on all issues in your case before mediation. Knowledge is power in your divorce, and with the legal guidelines of your chosen divorce lawyer and the mediator, you can decide between rolling the dice in a divorce trial or reaching a settlement.

3. Experienced Divorce Attorney Mediator

You made a wise investment in hiring the right divorce lawyer for your case. Hiring the most experienced mediator on the issues in your divorce is a smart investment as well. The Internet is a great tool for research, but it is also plagued with false advertisements for the "best divorce mediators" and the "best divorce lawyers." The adage of "you get what you pay for" is true in divorce litigation. Unfortunately, anyone can claim they are a divorce mediator. Therefore, it is in your best interest to hire an experienced divorce attorney or divorce law firm that will recommend the right divorce mediator for you and the issues in your case.

Some divorce mediators are highly skilled in resolving financial issues, others are better at child custody, and only a few are great for all issues. Issues as important as your divorce, the future of your children, and finances are too important to work with a cheap lawyer. Experience matters in divorce mediation; work with your divorce attorney to select the best mediator for your divorce.

4. Unbiased Experienced Opinion

Your chosen divorce attorney ensures the mediator working on your divorce case is fair in their approach to your case. An experienced and fair divorce mediator has no preconceived notions, other than experience in court, on the following issues: child custody, legal custody, child visitation, child support, alimony, division of property, division of debts, retirement accounts, and much more.

You should express your concerns to your divorce attorney if you fear the mediator in your divorce is biased against you. They may not be biased but providing you with an honest and unbiased opinion on what is likely to happen in court if you have a divorce trial.

High net worth divorcees or higher-earning spouses often assume that mediation is an avenue to maximize recovery in the divorce. However, this is not the case. You will save a lot of money and heartache by resolving your divorce at mediation, in lieu of the uncertainty of a divorce trial. However, do not expect the divorce mediator in your case to side unfairly in your favor. The unbiased or neutral opinion of an experienced divorce mediator is invaluable to reaching a positive and expedited resolution of your divorce. Speak to your chosen divorce lawyer about mediation and the benefits it may provide you in your specific divorce case.

Divorce mediation is a great tool in many divorces, but not all divorce cases, to obtain a clear idea of what may happen on the issues in your case in a divorce trial. Additionally, in many contested divorce cases, mediation results in the settlement of the case without trial. This section is a brief overview of divorce mediation; however, you should consider many more factors regarding participating in divorce mediation or foregoing the opportunity.

Contempt of Court

What Is Contempt of Court?

There are two types of contempt of court, and both occur in family law proceedings: direct contempt and indirect contempt. Direct contempt is disorderly or insolent behavior *during court session*. Indirect contempt is willful disobedience of a court process or any lawful order by the court.

What Is the Punishment for Contempt of Court?

The punishment for contempt in a family law, divorce, or custody proceeding may be remedial to convince or coerce the defendant to follow the court order, or it may be punitive to punish the defendant for failing to comply with a court order.

What Happens If I Correct the Basis for Contempt?

Generally, if you correct the issue raised in the contempt action, your family law attorney must either convince the other side of your divorce or child custody case to discuss the contempt action or convince the judge to dismiss based on your correcting the issue raised in the contempt action.

What Defenses Are There to Contempt?

There are a number of defenses to contempt of court in family law, divorce, or custody proceedings, including but not limited to the following:

- the violation was not willful,
  - for example, the child support or alimony payment was not made because the party was unable to make the payment;
- the alleged contemptuous act is not in violation of a court order,

- o for example, the conduct violated an agreement between the parties but not part of the divorce decree, custody plan, or a temporary order of the court;
- the contempt may be purged by correcting the act in contempt of court,
  - o for example, paying back child support or support alimony or returning the property agreed in a divorce decree or temporary order;
- the defendant is not at fault for the contempt,
  - o for example, the defendant's inability to comply was due to factors outside the defendant's control, such as a third party possessing the property that the divorce court's temporary order required to be turned over to the other party;
- statute of limitations has run on the act in the divorce action, which was contemptuous; or
- you did not receive proper notice of the contempt in your family law matter or divorce.

What Can I Do If the Other Party Introduces Issues at a Contempt Hearing?

The court should not consider issues outside the petition or amended petition for contempt unless the parties agree to those issues decided at one time. The court does not have the authority to render judgment in a contempt case, even in a divorce or child custody proceeding, without proper notice of a contempt action provided to the defendant.

Can You Appeal Family Court Decisions?

Yes, you can appeal a family court decision. When a person or family considers an appeal from a family court decision, they are likely very frustrated with an outcome at the trial court level. To effectively initiate a family law court appeal, multiple specific steps must be met on a specific timeline for appellate courts to have jurisdiction over your divorce or family court proceeding.

Family Court Appeals

This information is only a cursory examination of the process for considering and filing a family law court appeal. This summary applies only to family law court or civil court appeals. Each necessary step in the process of a family law appeal is discussed briefly; however, for more specific information, you should speak to an experienced family law appellate attorney.

Do You Have Grounds for a Family Law Appeal?

Unfortunately, not liking the judge's decision in your family law trial or divorce trial is not a valid basis for relief on appeal. However, if the family law judge misinterpreted the law or another error occurred in your family law trial, you may be entitled to relief on appeal.

The following are the most common bases for an appeal in a divorce trial or family law trial. Keep in mind that this list is not exhaustive; however, it covers most of the appellate issues that warrant relief in family law appeals:

- Misapplication of the Law
- Constitutional Violations
- Lack of Evidence to Support the Family Law Judge's Decision
- Abuse of Discretion by the Family Law Judge

- Wrong Evidentiary Rulings on Critical Points
- Failure to Properly Consider Best Interest of the Child Factors

Seek an Experienced Family Law Appeals Attorney

Not all divorce attorneys handle appeals since the process is complex and requires a type of written advocacy not common in divorce court or child custody cases. You need an experienced family law appeals attorney if you are seeking to overturn a district court judge's decision in your family law case.

Considerations Prior to Seeking an Appeal

You should meet with an experienced family law appellate attorney prior to filing any appeal from an adverse judgment in any family law proceeding. In some instances, you may ask the court to reconsider an issue; however, proceed cautiously. There is a serious risk of missing a procedural timeline to file an appeal if the court determines that your appeal was filed too long after the court's original order that you are seeking to appeal.

One important consideration in family law appeals is that you must raise *every* issue you want to preserve for appeal if you seek a new trial at the district court level. You can only raise issues on appeal that were in your motion for a new trial. Therefore, you should not only raise the issues in a motion for a new trial that you believe may warrant a new trial. Instead, you should raise every issue you have with the family law judge's initial ruling to preserve each issue on appeal.

The deadline to file your appeal is one of the most important considerations in what you do at the district court level prior to filing your family law appeal. Only certain issues raised in post-judgment motions extend your deadline to file an appeal. Most post-trial motions in family law cases do not extend your timeline. Failure to file your appeal on time bars your access to appellate review unless post-conviction relief is granted in the district court and the appellate court for failing to file your appeal on time. Granted or not, missing a deadline is not the best way to begin the family law appellate process.

Filing Your Family Law Court Appeal

The first step in filing a family law court appeal is preparing and filing your Petition in Error with the appellate court. It is the catalyst to the process of any appeal in a civil case. The Petition in Error is a document that summarizes the issues for review, explains the type of family law case on appeal, and generally outlines the issues and facts before the appellate court. Additionally, your Petition in Error for your family law appeal must explain the procedural posture, series of events, in your family law case.

Timing is critical to preserving your appeal, and, in most cases in Oklahoma, you have thirty days from the filing date of the challenged order with the district court. Identifying what constitutes the final order and starting the clock for your appeal is very important. Typically, the trial court minutes are insufficient to start the clock. However, you should speak to your family law appellate attorney to ensure you meet this deadline. Failure to file your Petition in Error by the deadline waives your right to appeal.

Compiling the Record

Appellate courts do not conduct a new trial or hear from witnesses. Rather, appellate courts review the transcripts and rulings from the family law trial or the district court record to reach their decision. Therefore, it is up to the party seeking an appeal to provide the family law appeals court with the record.

At the same time of your Petition in Error drafting and filing, your family law appellate attorney must file a Designation of Record at the trial court level. Your Designation of Record is how you "designate" or tell the district court clerk what transcripts, pleadings filed in the case, and orders of the court are necessary for appeal.

Additionally, the opposing party in your appeal, the Respondent, can provide a separate Designation of Record, which directs the district court clerk to compile any additional materials for appellate review, not identified by the appealing party.

All this to say, a well-built record is crucial to your chances for success on appeal, as the appellate court does not consider any additional or new evidence. Additionally, any hearings that took place relevant to your family law appeal cannot be considered unless there is a record of the proceedings. We advise you make a record with a court reporter at every hearing during your family law or divorce case. Also, court minutes and journal entries in your case are very specific because these court orders are subject to appellate review.

Once you file your Designation of the Record with the district court clerk, the clerk's office has six months to compile the record for appeal in your family law appeal. The appellant, the party bringing the appeal, is responsible for ensuring the clerk completes the record on time. Therefore, you want to ensure the family law appellate attorney you work with stays in contact with the clerk's office. Additionally, the appellant is responsible for ensuring all court reporters that transcribed a proceeding in the Designation of Record receive the Designation of Record and draft the transcripts on time, which usually requires paying for the transcript before the work is done.

The Briefing Process

Once the Petition in Error and Designation of Record discussed above are filed, it is time to start briefing the appeal. It is best practice to immediately begin outlining and researching for the appeal, even though you do not yet have the transcript to cite to the record.

For example, in Oklahoma, you only have sixty days once the record is complete, as the Appellant seeking relief on appeal, to finish and file your brief in chief. The brief in chief is your best opportunity to explain to the appellate court what errors occurred at the trial court level in your family law case, warranting relief from the appellate court.

Once the appellant's brief in chief is filed, the respondent or appellee has forty days to file an answer brief. The answer brief, or response brief, is the most important pleading by the respondent to the appeal since you are not entitled to a second brief unless permitted by the court.

In most cases, the final brief is a reply brief by the appellant who brought the appeal. Although you are entitled to file a reply brief, it is not always wise to do so. When you have made your best points in your opening brief, you should not waste the appellate court's time by repeating yourself. You should only file a reply brief if the respondent mentions an issue or argument that you believe warrants a reply.

Finally, in very few cases, the appellate court in your family case may grant the respondent a sur reply, which is a second opportunity to submit a brief by the respondent. You should speak to an experienced appellate family law attorney before seeking permission for a sur reply.

Assignment and Opinion

The appellate court to which your appeal is assigned depends on state appellate law. In many cases, the appellate review is done by a panel of judges. Together, they review all the briefs, decide the case, and draft an opinion on the issues on appeal.

The opinion in your family law case appeal either affirms the family law trial court's decision or overturns the decision with instructions for the district court to enter the appropriate new court orders, dictated by the appellate court. Although parties appealing a family law decision have strict timelines to submit pleadings and procedural matters, the appellate court is not bound by any timelines. Therefore, the next step is waiting for the court to issue the opinion in your family law appeal.

Additional Appeals in Family Law Cases

In addition to the process discussed above, you are entitled to "ask for review" by the highest state court if the decision on appeal is averse to you. The process to seek additional appellate review in a family law case is the same as any other civil case; you must file a writ of certiorari to the highest state court (usually called the Supreme Court – though not in all states). Additionally, you may ask the court that heard your appeal to reconsider its decision.

On certiorari, the highest state court has complete discretion to "grant cert" and review your case or deny your request and close your appeal. In cases where the highest court elects to grant certiorari, the court either affirms or reverses the intermediate appellate court's decision.

Finally, if you are granted certiorari and receive an outcome that you are not satisfied with, you have ninety days to seek additional review by the highest state court if you have grounds to do so. Once you have exhausted state court remedies, you may seek review by the United States Supreme Court; however, this is again discretionary certiorari review: hardly ever granted. Therefore, you should consult an experienced appellate family law attorney before seeking certiorari.

Final Opinion

Once all avenues of relief are exhausted, including the time to file a request for reconsideration or a writ for certiorari, the highest state court issues a mandate in your case. The mandate is the order returning your case to the trial court for the lower court to implement the orders of the appellate court and, if necessary, additional proceedings. Most people are not aware; however, the ruling of the appellate court, for instance, a favorable opinion on your behalf, is not in force or effect until the mandate is issued. You may take comfort in winning your family law appeal; however, it is not the order of the court until all review is exhausted and the mandate has been issued.

Family Law Appeals Process Conclusion

The rules and procedures that govern family law appeals are strict; however, by working with an experienced family law appeals attorney, you stand the best chance of complying with all the rules to ensure your appeal is heard and to present the strongest argument possible in your case.

CONCLUSION—MOVING FORWARD

"Awesome staff, really hard-working and passionate folks. Made me feel like someone had my back during a really difficult time in my life, and Jodi in particular has been nothing but awesome!"

Phillip

I have seen divorce from many angles throughout my life: my parent's divorce from each other and from subsequent spouses, my friends and colleagues, and countless clients. In their lives, I have seen time and time again that those facing divorce with courage and knowledge of the issues and the process fare far better than those who are timid and refuse to educate themselves. I sincerely hope this book has educated you on the process and the issues you are likely to face in your divorce. Absorbing the information in this book will not make divorce easy. Along the way, you will certainly encounter emotional, mental, or spiritual difficulties, and you may face financial challenges. Fear is a normal biological response to facing the unknown or experiences that are unfamiliar, such as divorce.

You may find yourself saying, "this process will never end" or "I'm not strong enough to get through this divorce," but you are wrong on both accounts. *The divorce process will come to a resolution, and you are strong enough to get through your divorce* I wrote this book because I believe that *knowledge is power.* Thanks to this written guide, you now have a better understanding of the road ahead you; armed with this knowledge, *you will be better prepared to face it whatever your specific divorce may bring.*

Whatever your greatest fear in your divorce, you can develop a plan and strategy to be courageous and overcome it. We encourage you to work with experienced divorce counsel that you Know, Like, and Trust in this very stressful time. You should not walk this road alone or with an attorney that is not prepared to be Your Fierce Advocate®.

Whether you live in Oklahoma or not, whether you decide to work with Cannon & Associates or not, please find divorce counsel capable of walking beside you to the finish line or carrying you if necessary. You are strong enough to outlast divorce, and we stand ready to be Your Fierce Advocates® and your personal guide through this process.

You will survive your divorce. You will have a life after divorce. You can find love after divorce. You will have a relationship with your children after divorce. Trust me on the last point; I know from firsthand experience. After my parents got divorced when I was in middle school, my relationship with both parents changed. It may surprise you when I say that I had a *better* relationship with both. I spent one-on-one time with each of my parents and grew closer to each of them as a result. Your life will look and feel different until not being married to your former spouse becomes normal again.

Take comfort knowing that your divorce shall pass. Remember, you can do all things through Him who gives you strength. All you need to do is ask. You *can* have a fulfilling life after divorce; it is your choice. You will have a fulfilling life after divorce if you inform yourself about your rights, ask for what you want, and seek guidance from experienced counsel. We wish you the best on the road you're walking and beyond.

ACKNOWLEDGEMENTS

"The team at Cannon and Associates have been very helpful and professional. They have kept me up to date on matters and have helped in guiding me the right direction to move forward."

Garth

We would like to express our gratitude to you for taking the time to read this book and educate yourself with *Informed Divorce*. Our firm is dedicated to being Fierce Advocates® for the clients and families we have the privilege to serve. You have taken the first step to the rest of your life and **Your Better Future Now**. Whether we are the right fit for your or not, we would be glad to meet with you, answer your questions, and show you how you can begin **Your Better Future Now**.

I am thankful for a deep and profound faith in God, which continually shapes my life and how I try to interact with the world. My amazing wife, Megan. She is a bright light in my life, my inspiration, and is always there to support me and our family. Thank you to my three beautiful children, you bring so much joy to the world and remind me every day why it is so important to fight for the benefit and happiness of children in family court.

To the amazing team in our office that works for the benefit of our clients day in and day out, you change lives for the better.

TESTIMONIALS

"I recently called Cannon & Associates seeking legal advice. All of my questions were well received and answered very knowledgeably by Kelly. The office is beautiful, everyone is very respect and courteous, as well as extremely knowledgeable and professional. I would highly recommend this law firm to anyone."

Kasey

"The receptionist was very professional and polite. My attorney had my case tied up in no time. A big shout out to Angelia Clark for the referral."

MJ

"Very helpful and patient. I didn't know what to expect but they assured me that I made the right choice. Thank you guys, and I will recommend you to anyone I know."

Kurt

"Everyone at this firm is outstanding! Very Professional and Respectful People! From the very beginning they treated me with Respect and took my case serious! The outcome for me was better than I ever expected!!"

Kenneth

35. Temporary orders.

* 59 - Write down goals. ~ talk to Peter
  about them

94 - Dress well.

148 - The Parties Contributions

195 -

196 -

197

Made in the USA
Las Vegas, NV
02 November 2022

58613726R00132